THE HISTORY OF MAJOR LEAGUE BASEBALL

A Chronicle of MLB's Evolution, Legendary Moments, and the Rich Tapestry of Baseball History

James Bren

Chapters

Introduction: A Journey Through the History of Major League Baseball

Nestled within the very soul of the American spirit lies a storied tapestry, woven with threads of triumph, defeat, legends, and an undying passion that has stood the test of time. Welcome, dear reader, to the expansive pages of "The Grand Slam Chronicles: A Journey Through the History of Major League Baseball." Prepare yourself for an extraordinary odyssey that transcends the boundaries of mere chronicles, unveiling the awe-inspiring saga of a sport that has not only captured the imaginations but also claimed the hearts of millions around the globe.

Our narrative begins in the heartland of organized baseball during the mid-19th century, a time when the crack of the bat echoed through bustling urban streets and across the sprawling fields of the rural Midwest. From these humble origins, legendary franchises emerged, and iconic players etched their names into the annals of history, while the foundations of time-honored traditions were laid. The evolution of America's national pastime unfolds before us, a mosaic intricately intertwined with the cultural, social, and political landscapes of the nation itself.

This is not a mere recitation of scores and statistics; it is a jubilant celebration of the human spirit and the indomitable will to succeed. Each chapter unveils the highs of record-breaking victories and the lows of heart-wrenching defeats, delving into the stories behind the box scores. We uncover the triumphs of underdogs, the camaraderie forged in dugouts, and the unwavering commitment of players who, through their exploits, became larger-than-life figures in the collective imagination of fans.

As we traverse through the decades, we explore transformative moments that forever altered the course of MLB history—the shattering of barriers, the league's expansion, and the globalization of the game. From the iconic "Shot Heard 'Round the World" to the infamous "Curse of the Bambino," each chapter unfolds as a riveting tale, inviting readers to relive the excitement and drama that have, for generations, defined baseball as more than just a sport; it's a cultural phenomenon that reflects the heartbeat of a nation.

"The Grand Slam Chronicles" extends a heartfelt invitation for you to step into the cleats of the players, feel the palpable anticipation in the air during the World Series, and bear witness to the evolution of baseball as it mirrors the evolving identity of the nation it so faithfully represents. So, fasten your seatbelts, grab your peanuts and crackerjacks, and join us as we embark on an immersive and captivating journey through the bases, celebrating the enduring legacy of Major League Baseball.

Chapter 1: The Birth Pangs: Unveiling the Genesis of a National Passion

In the tumultuous landscape of the 1860s, amid the echoes of the Civil War, an unexpected beacon of unity emerged—baseball. As soldiers sought solace in the camaraderie of the game played in camps, "New York"-style baseball transcended its regional roots, evolving into a national pastime that would captivate the hearts of a divided nation. The simple joy of the sport became a unifying force, providing a sense of normalcy and shared experience amidst the chaos of war.

The Civil War, with its devastating toll on the nation, created a yearning for connections that transcended the battlefield. Baseball, with its accessible and communal nature, emerged as a salve for the wounds of war. Soldiers from both sides found a common ground on the diamond, engaging in friendly matches that briefly transported them away from the grim realities of conflict. The seeds of a national passion were sown as the crack of the bat and the thud of the ball against the glove echoed across military encampments.

The Dawn of Order: National Association of Base Ball Players (NABBP)

The need for order in the aftermath of the war led to the establishment of the National Association of Base Ball Players (NABBP) in 1858. This marked the first step toward organizing the burgeoning passion for baseball. The NABBP became the sport's inaugural governing body, bringing standardization to rules, fostering fair competition, and providing a framework for a community of players across the nation. This organizational effort not only provided structure to the game but also laid the foundation for the future growth and development of baseball as a nationwide phenomenon.

In the wake of the war, there was a palpable desire for normalcy and routine. Baseball, through the NABBP, provided a sense of order and structure. The NABBP's mission went beyond simply codifying the rules; it aimed to create a sense of community among baseball enthusiasts. The association's formation marked a departure from the informal and often chaotic nature of early baseball games to a more regulated and organized sport. This transition was vital in transforming baseball from a casual amusement to a serious and respected pastime.

A Decade of Amateurism: NABBP's Formative Years

For a significant span of twelve years, the NABBP operated as an amateur league. It served as a hub for enthusiasts, boasting over 400 member clubs by 1867. This period solidified baseball's status as a national pastime, with its roots firmly embedded in the diverse fabric of American communities. However, despite the widespread participation, the Northeastern United States remained the nucleus of baseball's strength, housing the most formidable and influential clubs. The amateur era was characterized by a spirit of camaraderie and love for the game, laying the groundwork for the fervor that would follow in the years to come.

The NABBP's embrace of amateurism fostered a sense of inclusivity within the baseball community. Clubs, ranging from small townships to bustling cities, found a common ground under the NABBP's umbrella. This period witnessed a democratization of the sport, with enthusiasts from various backgrounds coming together to play a game that transcended social divides. The amateur ethos, far from being a limitation, became a strength, creating a vibrant tapestry of baseball experiences across the nation.

Northeastern Dominance: The Heartland of Baseball

Cities like New York, Philadelphia, and Boston emerged as the epicenters of baseball prowess. The Northeast, with its concentration of robust clubs, became synonymous with excellence in the sport. This regional dominance not only showcased a commitment to baseball but also contributed to shaping a distinctive baseball culture. The strongholds in the Northeast became crucibles of talent, where rivalries were forged, and the competitive spirit of baseball thrived. It was within this vibrant baseball culture that the foundations of the professional game were laid.

The Northeast's ascendancy in baseball was not merely geographical; it was a testament to the region's dedication to the sport. Cities became battlegrounds, and rivalries turned into epic showdowns that captivated local communities. The fervor for baseball reached a fever pitch, and the clubs from the Northeast set the standards for excellence, inspiring generations of players and fans alike. The Northeastern dominance, far from isolating the sport, became a driving force behind its nationwide appeal.

The Birth of Professionalism: Cincinnati Red Stockings

The transformative moment arrived in 1869 with the birth of professional play. The Cincinnati Red Stockings, under the guidance of Harry Wright, etched their name in history as the first professional baseball team. This marked a paradigm shift, as players transitioned from amateurs driven by passion to professionals earning their livelihood through the sport. The Red Stockings not only pioneered professionalism but also set an enduring standard of excellence that would resonate through the ages, heralding the dawn of a new era for baseball. This shift to professionalism marked a crucial juncture, as baseball evolved from a local pastime to a nationally celebrated sport, forever altering the trajectory of its storied history.

The Cincinnati Red Stockings, with their groundbreaking move to professionalism, represented more than a shift in the way baseball was played; they symbolized a changing societal view towards sports and entertainment. The Red Stockings became trailblazers, demonstrating that baseball could be a viable profession. This move paved the way for a new era of baseball, where players could dedicate themselves fully to the sport, leading to increased competition, higher skill levels, and an ever-growing fanbase.

Chapter 2: Rupture and Renaissance: Birth of Professionalism

In the aftermath of the Cincinnati Red Stockings' daring venture into professionalism in 1869, a schism rippled through the baseball community, shaping the course of the sport's evolution. The ideological divide between those embracing baseball as a livelihood and those adhering to its amateur roots became more pronounced. The tension escalated, prompting a pivotal moment in the history of baseball—the split of the National Association of Base Ball Players (NABBP) into distinct professional and amateur factions.

The Birth of the National Association (NA): 1871

Amidst the fissures, the National Association of Professional Base Ball Players, commonly known as the National Association (NA), emerged in 1871 as the vanguard of the professional movement. This marked the formalization of baseball as a paid profession, setting the stage for the structured leagues that would follow. The NA laid down the framework for organized professional play, introducing a level of competition and spectacle that captivated fans and players alike. The birth of the NA was a watershed moment, signaling the irrevocable shift towards baseball as a burgeoning industry.

The Vanishing Amateur Counterpart

While the professional ranks flourished, the amateur counterpart within the NABBP faced a different fate. The amateur organization, unable to withstand the rising tide of professionalism, faded into obscurity after only a few years. The dominance of professional play signaled a cultural shift, as baseball transformed from a pastime played for the love of the game into a professional pursuit. The disappearance of the amateur faction within the NABBP marked the end of an era, making way for the ascendance of organized, professional baseball.

Legacies Woven: Chicago Cubs and Atlanta Braves

Amidst the upheaval, the legacies of two iconic franchises, the modern Chicago Cubs and Atlanta Braves, find their roots in the National Association of Professional Base Ball Players in the 1870s. These franchises, now storied pillars of Major League Baseball, trace their lineage back to the early days of professional play. The Chicago Cubs, born as the Chicago White Stockings, and the Atlanta Braves, initially the Boston Red Stockings, were among the pioneering clubs that navigated the uncharted waters of the NA.

The Chicago Cubs, with a history that intertwines with the very foundations of professional baseball, evolved from the White Stockings of the NA to become a symbol of resilience and triumph. The team weathered the changes of time, celebrated victories, and endured challenges, creating a narrative that mirrors the ebb and flow of baseball's evolution.

Similarly, the Atlanta Braves, originating as the Boston Red Stockings in the NA, embarked on a journey that spans decades. The Braves' saga reflects the resilience of a franchise tethered to the earliest days of professional play. Through relocations and rebranding, the Braves preserved a connection to their historic roots, embodying the enduring spirit of a team forged in the crucible of the National Association.

The Impact of the Schism: Shaping the Future

The schism between professional and amateur ballplayers, culminating in the formation of the National Association, left an indelible mark on the trajectory of baseball. The embrace of professionalism brought with it a new era of competition, strategy, and spectatorship. As the professional game gained momentum, drawing larger audiences and cultivating fervent fanbases, it laid the groundwork for the structured leagues that would follow.

The rupture within the NABBP was not merely a divide between players but a seismic shift that resonated through the entire baseball landscape. The advent of professionalism transformed baseball from a local and regional pastime into a national spectacle, with players becoming not just representatives of their communities but also professionals with a broader fan following.

As the Chicago Cubs and Atlanta Braves emerged as torchbearers of the NA legacy, they became living testimonials to the resilience and adaptability that define the essence of baseball. The schism, while initially divisive, sowed the seeds of a more expansive and inclusive era for the sport. The legacy of the National Association continues to echo through the decades, reminding us that every crack in the foundation of the old can give rise to the enduring structures of the new.

Chapter 3: Birth of Stability: The National League Era

In the transformative year of 1876, a pivotal moment in the history of baseball unfolded—the establishment of the National League of Professional Base Ball Clubs. This league, later known simply as the National League or NL, emerged as the remedy to the perceived inefficacy of its predecessor, the National Association (NA). The NL, founded on principles of stability and structure, laid down the groundwork for the enduring institution that is Major League Baseball.

Emphasis on Clubs: Shifting the Paradigm

Unlike the NA, which struggled with a player-centric focus, the National League shifted its emphasis to the clubs themselves. This marked a fundamental change in the organizational philosophy, as the league recognized the importance of creating stable and competitive teams. By placing the spotlight on the clubs, the NL introduced a framework that would endure for decades, shaping the identity and dynamics of professional baseball.

The NL's approach allowed clubs to enforce player contracts, a significant departure from the NA era. This move prevented players from freely jumping to higher-paying clubs, providing a level playing field for teams and fostering a sense of loyalty among players. The newfound stability paved the way for the cultivation of team identities and the rise of fan allegiances, essential elements in the evolution of baseball as a national pastime.

A Commitment to Complete Schedules: Fostering Fair Competition

One of the NL's groundbreaking innovations was the requirement for clubs to play the full schedule of games. This was in stark contrast to the NA, where forfeited games were a common occurrence, especially when a club found itself out of contention for the league championship. The NL's insistence on completing the schedule introduced a sense of integrity to the competition, ensuring that every game had relevance and impact on the overall standings.

The commitment to completing schedules not only elevated the competitiveness of the league but also contributed to the growth of fan engagement. Fans now had a consistent and reliable season to follow, and the suspense of a full schedule added a layer of drama that captivated audiences. This shift laid the groundwork for the enduring drama of pennant races and the thrill of the postseason that would become synonymous with Major League Baseball.

Curbing Gambling: Restoring the Integrity of the Game

A significant challenge faced by early baseball was the influence of gambling on game outcomes, casting doubts on the validity of results. Recognizing the importance of preserving the integrity of the sport, the National League made a concerted effort to curb gambling. This initiative aimed to ensure that the outcomes of games were determined solely by the skill and performance of the players on the field, untainted by external influences.

The NL's stand against gambling marked a turning point in the perception of baseball as a legitimate and honorable pursuit. By addressing this issue head-on, the league not only restored confidence in the authenticity of results but also contributed to the establishment of baseball as a sport that could be trusted and revered by fans.

Inaugural Game: April 22, 1876—The Birth of MLB

The first game in the National League, played on Saturday, April 22, 1876, at the Jefferson Street Grounds in Philadelphia, is often pointed to as the official beginning of Major League Baseball (MLB). This historic moment symbolized the culmination of years of experimentation and evolution, as the

NA ushered in an era of stability, structure, and professionalization.

As the crack of the bat echoed through the Jefferson Street Grounds, a new chapter in the history of baseball unfolded. The NL's inaugural game was more than a contest between two teams; it was a declaration that baseball had come of age as a professional and organized sport. The significance of this moment reverberates through the annals of MLB history, as the league became the standard-bearer for the sport's future.

Chapter 4: From Turmoil to Triumph: The Evolution of Professional Baseball

The early years of the National League (NL) were marked by turbulence, as the fledgling league navigated threats from rival organizations and internal strife among players. A particular source of discontent was the infamous "reserve clause," a contentious element that restricted the free movement of players between clubs. This clause became a focal point of rebellion, with players seeking to break free from its constraints and assert their autonomy in a league where power dynamics were still finding equilibrium.

Ebb and Flow: Teams in Flux

The stability that the NL sought to establish was elusive in its formative years. Teams entered and exited the league with remarkable frequency. It wasn't until 1882 that the league witnessed its first season with the same membership as the preceding year. The transient nature of franchises underscored the challenges of maintaining a stable and enduring league, with only four teams persevering to see the dawn of the 20th century.

The constant turnover in teams mirrored the competitive environment of the era. Rival leagues regularly formed and disbanded, vying for attention and legitimacy. Amid this tumult, one league stood out—the American Association (AA), often colloquially referred to as the "beer and whiskey league" for its lenient stance on the sale of alcoholic beverages to spectators.

Brewing Rivalries: NL vs. American Association

The American Association, in existence from 1882 to 1891, became the most formidable competitor to the National League. Its laissez-faire attitude towards alcohol sales, combined with a willingness to experiment with game formats, drew significant fan interest. For several years, champions from the NL and the AA faced off in a postseason championship series—an early precursor to what would later become the World Series.

This period witnessed the birth pangs of interleague competition, providing fans with a taste of the excitement that would define the pinnacle of baseball championships. The rivalry between the NL and the AA not only fueled competition but also prompted innovations, setting the stage for the evolution of professional baseball as a spectacle that captivated the masses.

Merging Paths: The Union of NL and AA

Recognizing the need for unity in the face of constant upheaval, the National League and the American Association merged in 1892. The union created a single, formidable 12-team National League, seeking to consolidate talent and stabilize the baseball landscape. However, this consolidation was short-lived, as the NL dropped four teams after the 1899 season.

This contraction paved the way for a new chapter in baseball history—the formation of the American League (AL) in 1901. Under the presidency of Ban Johnson, the American League emerged as a distinct entity, sparking a bidding war for players that reverberated through the baseball world. This period of intense competition saw widespread contract-breaking and legal disputes, challenging the very foundations of player-team relationships.

Bidding Wars and Legal Turmoil: The Birth of the American League

The American League's inception in 1901 triggered a new era of competition, not just on the field but also in the negotiation rooms. The bidding war for players, driven by the charismatic leadership of Ban Johnson, unfolded as a high-stakes battle for talent. This fierce competition led to a wave of contract-breaking, as players sought better deals and teams fought for the brightest stars.

The legal disputes that ensued marked a period of uncertainty and reevaluation of the contractual framework within professional baseball. The turmoil surrounding player contracts became a battleground for defining the rights and responsibilities of both players and clubs. This era laid the groundwork for the eventual establishment of a more structured and regulated system that would govern player-team relationships.

Chapter 5: The Turbulent Symphony: The War Between Leagues and the Birth of the National Association

The dawn of the 20th century marked a tumultuous period in the baseball world as the war between the American League (AL) and the National League (NL) sent shockwaves through the sport. The fierce competition for players, fan loyalty, and territorial dominance ignited a conflict that would redefine the landscape of professional baseball. In the midst of this upheaval, a pivotal meeting at the Leland Hotel in Chicago in 1901 would shape the destiny of baseball leagues and set the stage for the birth of the National Association.

The Leland Hotel Summit: Negotiating Independence

In 1901, baseball's power brokers convened at the Leland Hotel in Chicago, acutely aware that the war between the AL and NL had far-reaching implications for the entire baseball ecosystem. This historic meeting brought together representatives from various baseball leagues, each grappling with the challenge of maintaining independence in the face of the escalating rivalry between the major leagues.

The Leland Hotel summit became a crucible for negotiation, compromise, and strategic planning.

The representatives recognized the need for a unified front to protect the interests of minor leagues and preserve the integrity of baseball beyond the major league battleground. As a result, a visionary plan began to take shape, one that would lay the foundation for the autonomy and coexistence of baseball leagues.

Rise of the National Association: Guardian of Minor Leagues

In response to the escalating conflict, the baseball leagues outside the AL and NL orchestrated a groundbreaking move—the formation of the National Association. This new governing body, distinct from its 19th-century predecessor, was tasked with overseeing and regulating the minor leagues. Its mission was clear: to provide a structured framework for the development and operation of minor league baseball, ensuring that it thrived independently of the major league skirmish.

The National Association's role extended beyond mere oversight; it became a guardian of the minor leagues' interests. As major league powers clashed, the National Association worked to maintain a delicate balance, offering a refuge for leagues seeking stability amid the storm. It emerged as a symbol of unity, resilience, and a commitment to the enduring spirit of baseball at all levels.

Navigating the Storm: Minor Leagues in the AL-NL Crossfire

While the AL and NL battled for supremacy, the minor leagues found themselves caught in the crossfire. The recruiting wars, player raids, and territorial disputes between the major leagues threatened the very existence of these smaller entities. The National Association, born out of necessity, became a shield against the storm, providing a collective voice for the minor leagues and a platform for collaboration.

The minor leagues, under the umbrella of the National Association, adopted a strategy of solidarity. By banding together, they could resist the encroachments of the major leagues and fortify themselves against the challenges of an ever-changing baseball landscape. The National Association became a beacon of hope, ensuring that the rich tapestry of baseball, woven through the efforts of countless communities, remained intact.

Legacy of Independence: Minor Leagues Flourish

The creation of the National Association not only shielded the minor leagues from the turbulence of the AL-NL war but also laid the groundwork for their sustained growth. With a unified approach, minor leagues thrived, cultivating local talent, building fanbases, and contributing to the cultural fabric of countless towns and cities.

The legacy of independence forged by the National Association endures in the vibrant tapestry of minor league baseball. These leagues, no longer mere satellites of the major leagues, became integral components of the baseball ecosystem, fostering a love for the game in regions far removed from the bright lights of the major league stadiums.

The Leland Legacy: A Testament to Baseball's Resilience

The meeting at the Leland Hotel in Chicago stands as a testament to the resilience of baseball. In the face of internal strife threatening to unravel the very foundations of the sport, the baseball community demonstrated its capacity to adapt, negotiate, and forge solutions that would allow the game to transcend the challenges of its time.

The National Association, born from the crucible of conflict, became a guardian of baseball's future. It ensured that the essence of the game, with its roots in communities across the nation, could withstand the storms generated by the power struggles of the major leagues. The legacy of the Leland Hotel summit endures as a reminder that, even in the face of wars between titans, the heartbeat of baseball perseveres in the collective spirit of those who cherish the game.

Chapter 6: Forging Alliances: The National Agreement and the Birth of the Modern Minor League System

After the tumultuous years of conflict between the American League (AL) and the National League (NL), and the establishment of the National Association (NA) to safeguard the interests of minor leagues, the baseball world found itself at a crossroads. The need for stability and a clear framework for the coexistence of major and minor leagues led to a pivotal moment—the signing of the new National Agreement in 1902. This agreement would not only redefine the relationships between major and minor leagues but also lay the groundwork for the modern minor league system.

Ties that Bind: The National Agreement of 1902

In a bid to bring order to the chaos that had defined baseball in the early 20th century, representatives from the NL, AL, and NA came together to sign the National Agreement of 1902. This landmark accord aimed to establish a more structured and harmonious relationship between major and minor leagues. One of the key provisions of the agreement was the entwining of independent contracts with the reserve-clause contracts, creating a symbiotic link that would govern player movement and team affiliations.

The National Agreement of 1902 represented a collective commitment to the future of professional baseball, emphasizing cooperation over competition. By creating a framework that clarified the relationships between leagues and players, the agreement sought to bring stability to a sport that had been marked by turmoil and uncertainty in the preceding years.

The Birth of Classification: A System Takes Shape

Crucially, the National Agreement of 1902 introduced a formal classification system for minor leagues. This marked a significant departure from the ad-hoc arrangements that had characterized the minor league landscape. The classification system aimed to organize and standardize the structure of minor leagues, providing a clear hierarchy that would facilitate player development, team affiliations, and the overall coherence of the baseball ecosystem.

Branch Rickey, a visionary executive and innovator, would later refine and perfect this classification system. His contributions to baseball administration would leave an indelible mark on the sport, ensuring that the minor league structure evolved to become an integral part of the player development pipeline.

Ties that Bind: The Dual Contracts System

The entwining of independent contracts with reserve-clause contracts under the National Agreement of 1902 marked a paradigm shift in player-team relationships. This dual contracts system linked players to both major and minor league teams, providing a mechanism for the controlled movement of players within the baseball hierarchy.

For players, this system introduced a more defined career trajectory. Aspiring professionals could progress through the ranks of the minor leagues, honing their skills and gaining experience under the umbrella of major league affiliations. The dual contracts system not only brought stability to player careers but also ensured a steady flow of talent into the major leagues, contributing to the overall competitiveness and sustainability of the sport.

Rickey's Refinement: The Architect of the Modern Minor League System

Branch Rickey, a pioneering figure in baseball management, played a crucial role in refining and advancing the classification system introduced in the National Agreement of 1902. Rickey recognized the potential of the minor leagues as a fertile ground for talent development, and he sought to optimize their role in the larger baseball landscape.

Rickey's innovations included the establishment of farm systems, where major league teams would have direct affiliations with minor league clubs at various levels. This allowed for a more seamless transition of players from the minor leagues to the majors, ensuring a steady supply of skilled professionals. Rickey's visionary approach to player development laid the foundation for the modern minor league system, becoming an integral part of the player development pipeline that is still in place today.

Legacy of Stability: The Enduring Impact

The National Agreement of 1902 and its subsequent refinement by visionaries like Branch Rickey ushered in an era of stability and structure for professional baseball. The formal classification system for minor leagues, with its roots in this agreement, created a pathway for aspiring players to navigate their careers, while major league teams benefited from a streamlined player development process.

The enduring impact of the National Agreement is evident in the seamless coordination between major and minor league baseball today. The cooperative framework established over a century ago has stood the test of time, evolving into a sophisticated system that continues to fuel the growth and success of professional baseball. As the ties between major and minor leagues remain strong, the legacy of the National Agreement of 1902 endures as a testament to the enduring power of collaboration in shaping the future of the sport.

Chapter 7: Beyond the Duopoly: Exploring Other Recognized Leagues

In the vast mosaic of baseball history, the National League (NL) and the American League (AL) stand tall as foundational pillars. Yet, to encapsulate the richness of the sport, acknowledging other leagues is essential. Major League Baseball's (MLB) recognition of six additional major leagues in 1969 expanded the narrative, weaving a tapestry that extends beyond the duopoly. This chapter aims to unravel the stories, debates, and significance surrounding these leagues.

The Official Acknowledgment: The Special Baseball Records Committee (1969)

The decision by the Special Baseball Records Committee in 1969 was a pivotal moment in recognizing the diverse chapters of baseball. By officially acknowledging the American Association, Union Association, Players' League, and Federal League as major leagues, MLB embraced a broader perspective on the evolution of the sport. This recognition not only honored the achievements of players and teams in these leagues but also deepened the connection between different eras of baseball history.

The Disputed Legacy: The National Association

The National Association, active from 1871 to 1875, occupies a unique space in baseball's timeline. While its major league status remains disputed, the inclusion of its statistics by certain reference websites reflects a commitment to preserving the entirety of baseball's legacy. The debate surrounding the National Association underscores the challenges of defining major league status and prompts ongoing exploration into the intricacies of baseball's early years.

The Union Association Debate: Nate Silver's Perspective

Nate Silver's skepticism regarding the major league status of the Union Association adds a layer of complexity to the ongoing dialogue. By questioning factors beyond on-field performance, such as franchise stability and team ownership, Silver highlights the multifaceted nature of determining major league standing. This debate invites researchers and enthusiasts to delve into the historical context, raising questions about the criteria that define a league's place in baseball history.

The Negro Leagues: A Long-Awaited Recognition (2020–2021)

The belated recognition of seven Negro leagues as major leagues in 2020 marked a transformative moment in baseball history. MLB's acknowledgment and the subsequent inclusion of statistics by Baseball-Reference.com in 2021 represented a crucial step toward rectifying historical omissions. This move not only celebrated the exceptional talent that thrived in the Negro leagues but also signaled a commitment to a more inclusive and accurate representation of baseball's diverse heritage.

Unveiling the Layers: Beyond the Duopoly

Each league, whether officially recognized or subject to debate, has left an indelible mark on the evolution of baseball. Beyond the duopoly of the NL and AL, these leagues contributed to the sport's growth, introducing unique dynamics and narratives. The recognition of these layers enriches the collective understanding of America's pastime, encouraging fans and historians to explore the interconnected stories that have shaped the game we know today.

Conclusion: Embracing Baseball's Multifaceted Legacy

As MLB continues to embrace a more comprehensive view of its history, the acknowledgment of leagues beyond the NL and AL speaks to the complexity and inclusivity of baseball's legacy. Debates and discussions surrounding the major league status of certain leagues invite a deeper examination of the sport's evolution. By celebrating the diverse leagues that have contributed to the tapestry of Major League Baseball, we not only honor the past but also ensure a more vibrant and accurate portrayal of baseball's multifaceted legacy for future generations.

Chapter 8: The Dead-Ball Era: Pitcher's Paradise and Weathered Baseballs

The period spanning from 1900 to 1919 is etched in baseball history as the "dead-ball era." This unique epoch witnessed a distinctive style of play, characterized by . low-scoring games and a dominance of pitchers who became legends in their own right. Walter Johnson, Cy Young, Christy Mathewson, Mordecai Brown, and Grover Cleveland Alexander, among others, left an indelible mark on this era, shaping the narrative of baseball during a time when the sport's landscape and even the baseball itself underwent significant transformations.

The Pitching Pantheon: Dominance of Legends

Games of the dead-ball era were punctuated by pitching virtuosos whose mastery on the mound seemed unparalleled. Walter Johnson, known as the "Big Train," showcased an overpowering fastball that left batters flummoxed. Cy Young, a living legend whose name graces the annual award for pitching excellence, continued to etch his legacy. Christy Mathewson's surgical precision on the mound and Mordecai Brown's legendary curveball added depth to the pitching pantheon of this era. Grover Cleveland Alexander, with his intimidating presence, further solidified the dominance of pitchers during these years. The dead-ball era was a pitcher's paradise, and these hurlers stood as titans of their craft.

The Condition of the Baseball: A Game of Wear and Tear

The term "dead-ball" isn't just a nod to the low-scoring nature of the games; it accurately describes the condition of the baseball itself during this period. The baseball used American wool yarn, a far cry from the modern Australian wool, and was wound less tightly, affecting its trajectory and distance. However, the more significant impact lay in the longevity of the baseballs. Unlike today's pristine and frequently replaced baseballs, those of the dead-ball era endured wear and tear until they became mangled, soft, and sometimes lopsided. The reluctance of owners to purchase new balls, given their three-dollar cost (equivalent to $50.64 today, adjusted for inflation), contributed to a weathered, unpredictable playing experience.

Fan Involvement: Throwing Back Fouls and Home Runs

The dead-ball era wasn't just a spectacle on the field; fans played a participatory role. With the scarcity and cost of baseballs, fans were expected to throw back fouls and, on rare occasions, home runs hit into the stands. This interaction between players and fans added a dynamic element to the game, creating a unique bond between those on the field and those in the stands. The act of throwing back a ball wasn't just a ritual; it was a symbolic gesture, reflecting the scarcity and value attached to each baseball.

The Stained and Discolored Baseball: Tobacco Juice, Grass, and Licorice

The baseballs of the dead-ball era bore the scars of the game in more ways than one. Stained with tobacco juice, imprints of grass and mud, and sometimes even the residue of licorice, these baseballs told stories of on-field battles. Chewing licorice was not just a personal preference for some players; it served the purpose of discoloring the ball, creating an additional challenge for batters. The aesthetic wear and tear on the baseballs mirrored the grit and toughness required to navigate the dead-ball era.

Conclusion: Nostalgia and Legacy of the Dead-Ball Era

As we delve into the dead-ball era, a bygone chapter in baseball's chronicles, we encounter a unique blend of nostalgia and grit. The dominance of legendary pitchers, the weathered condition of the baseballs, fan involvement, and the stained, discolored artifacts of the game collectively paint a portrait of a bygone era. The dead-ball era wasn't just a period of low-scoring games; it was an era defined by the resilience of players, the connection between fans and the game, and the enduring legacy of those who mastered the nuances of baseball in its most distinctive form.

In the annals of baseball history, the dead-ball era stands as a testament to the sport's ability to evolve and adapt. The pitching prowess of legends and the unique characteristics of the baseball itself have left an indelible mark on the collective memory of baseball enthusiasts. As we reflect on this era, we find not just a period of statistical anomalies and low-scoring games, but a rich tapestry of stories that continue to resonate with the essence of America's pastime.

Chapter 9: Evolving Tactics and Ballpark Dimensions in the Golden Age

As the canvas of baseball unfolded into a new era, the game witnessed a profound metamorphosis, both in the strategic maneuvers enacted on the diamond and the physical dimensions that defined ballparks. Chapter 9 embarks on a comprehensive exploration of this transformative period, marked by the nuanced evolution of playing tactics and the distinctive challenges posed by the expansive ballparks.

The Spitball Era: Pitcher's Artistry Unleashed

In the early decades of the 20th century, pitchers ascended to a mythical status, wielding an unparalleled mastery over the baseball. It was during this era that the spitball emerged, a pitch that bore the fingerprints of a pitcher's artistry, subjecting the ball to a symphony of movements. By manipulating the ball with saliva or other substances, pitchers added an element of unpredictability, keeping batters perpetually guessing. The allure of the spitball reached its zenith, prompting the baseball authorities to intervene. In 1921, recognizing the need for regulation, the use of the spitball was curtailed and restricted to a select group of pitchers under a grandfather clause. This marked the end of an era but left an indelible legacy, symbolizing the ingenuity and creativity of pitchers in a bygone time.

Ballpark Dimensions: Where Size Matters

The physical dimensions of ballparks emerged as a silent architect, influencing the very fabric of the game. Akin to an artist selecting the right brushstroke, teams were confronted with expansive dimensions that favored finesse over power. Notable among these vast arenas were the West Side Grounds of the Chicago Cubs, with its center field fence positioned a staggering 560 feet away, and the Huntington Avenue Grounds of the Boston Red Sox, boasting a center field fence that stood an awe-inspiring 635 feet distant. These grandiose dimensions transformed the nature of play, where home runs became a cherished rarity, and the stage was set for the ascent of "small ball" strategies.

Small Ball Strategies: A Symphony of Singles and Bunts

The scarcity of home runs laid the foundation for an era where precision overshadowed power. Teams embraced the philosophy of "small ball," orchestrating a symphony of singles, bunts, stolen bases, and hit-and-run plays. The game evolved into a delicate dance where players, akin to skilled artisans, navigated the bases with finesse rather than brute force. The emphasis shifted from the mighty swing to the subtle maneuver, creating a strategic tapestry that encapsulated the essence of the Golden Age.

The Baltimore Chop: A Tactical Maneuver

Within this strategic renaissance, the Baltimore chop emerged as a distinctive brushstroke on the canvas of baseball tactics. Crafted to exploit the nuances of the infield and increase the tally of infield singles, this tactic showcased the inventive thinking of players. Executed with precision, the Baltimore chop involved the batter striking the ball forcefully into the ground, inducing a bounce of such elevation that reaching first base became a race against the flight of the ball. It epitomized the resourcefulness of players, adapting their approach to the ever-changing dynamics of the game.

Conclusion: The Golden Age Legacy

As we traverse the strategic landscapes of the Golden Age, where the spitball reigned and expansive ballparks dictated play, we unearth the intricate tapestry that defined this chapter in baseball's storied history. Pitchers, once maestros of the spitball, found their creativity curtailed but left an enduring legacy. Ballparks, with dimensions that favored finesse over power, birthed an era where "small ball" strategies flourished. The Baltimore chop and its ilk became tactical tools, emphasizing precision in a game where subtlety triumphed over sheer force. The legacy of the Golden Age endures, a testament to the adaptability of players and the perpetual evolution of strategies that continue to weave the timeless narrative of America's pastime.

Chapter 10: The Foul Strike Rule: Shifting Tides in Scoring Dynamics

The winds of change swept through the hallowed grounds of baseball in the early 20th century, bringing with them a transformative shift in the dynamics of scoring. Chapter 10 delves into a pivotal moment in the sport's evolution—the adoption of the foul strike rule. This seemingly minor alteration, implemented in the National League in 1901 and mirrored by the American League two years later, wielded a profound influence, morphing baseball from a high-scoring spectacle into a game where scoring runs became an arduous task. This chapter unravels the intricacies of this rule change and its far-reaching consequences on the delicate balance between pitchers and batters.

The Foul Strike Rule Unveiled: Counting the Strikes

In the years preceding the implementation of the foul strike rule, the batter enjoyed a significant advantage. Foul balls were not tallied as strikes, granting batters the liberty to foul off an unlimited number of pitches without accumulating any strikes against them. This unbridled opportunity to fend off pitches created a scenario where the batter held sway over the pitcher, tilting the balance in favor of scoring. However, winds of change were blowing, and baseball authorities recognized the need to level the playing field between pitcher and batter.

The National League Embraces Change (1901): The Dawn of a New Era

In 1901, the National League took the bold step of introducing the foul strike rule, marking a significant departure from the traditional scoring dynamics. Now, foul balls were incorporated into the strike count, restricting the batter's ability to accumulate an infinite number of foul balls without consequence. This alteration brought a sense of equilibrium, introducing a new layer of strategy and challenge into the batter-pitcher dynamic.

The American League Follows Suit (1903): A Unified Approach

Two years later, in 1903, the American League mirrored the National League's stance, adopting the foul strike rule. The unity in this rule's adoption across both major leagues signaled a recognition of its importance in refining the game's balance. The batter-pitcher duel, once heavily tilted in favor of the batter, now underwent a transformation, placing a premium on strategic shot selection and precise pitching.

Impact on Scoring Dynamics: A Pitcher's Renaissance

The repercussions of the foul strike rule reverberated across the diamond. The shift in scoring dynamics was palpable, as batters could no longer exploit the loophole of unlimited foul balls. Pitchers found themselves on a level playing field, empowered to use a more varied and strategic pitch selection without the constant threat of an unending barrage of fouls. This marked the dawn of a pitcher's renaissance, where precision and strategic acumen became paramount.

Strategies Redefined: Battling for Advantage

With foul balls now counting as strikes, batters were compelled to refine their strategies. The game became a mental chess match, with each pitch carrying added significance. Batters had to be more discerning, choosing when to unleash their full swing and when to employ a more defensive approach. Pitchers, on the other hand, could exploit this newfound vulnerability, testing batters with a diverse array of pitches designed to keep them off balance.

Challenges for Batters: Adapting to a New Reality

For batters, the adoption of the foul strike rule brought forth a formidable challenge. The days of freely fouling off pitches to extend at-bats were replaced by a more calculated approach. Batters had to adapt swiftly to this altered landscape, honing their ability to read pitches and make split-second decisions on when to swing, when to hold back, and when to unleash their power.

Conclusion: The Legacy of a Rule Change

As we reflect on the adoption of the foul strike rule, it becomes evident that this seemingly subtle alteration had far-reaching implications on the very essence of baseball. The transition from a high-scoring spectacle to a more strategic, hard-fought contest between pitcher and batter reshaped the narrative of the game. The unity between the National League and the American League in implementing this rule underscored its significance in leveling the playing field. The pitcher's renaissance, the redefined strategies of both batters and pitchers, and the challenges posed by this rule change created a new chapter in baseball's storied history. The legacy of the foul strike rule endures as a testament to the sport's continual evolution, where even the minutest adjustments can yield seismic shifts in the delicate equilibrium between tradition and progress.

Chapter 11: The Black Sox Scandal: A Stain on Baseball's Integrity

The aftermath of the 1919 World Series cast a dark and enduring shadow over the pristine field of baseball. Chapter 11 unearths the tumultuous events surrounding the Black Sox Scandal, a game-fixing scheme that stained the sport's integrity. The collusion of eight players, their intentional loss of the World Series, and the subsequent fallout forever altered the landscape of Major League Baseball.

The 1919 World Series: Prelude to Deceit

As the Chicago White Sox faced off against the Cincinnati Reds in the 1919 World Series, the stage was set for an unprecedented betrayal of the game. The clash between these two teams would not only determine a champion but also become the breeding ground for a sinister plot that would shake the foundations of baseball. Little did the fans and the baseball community know that the events about to unfold would scar the sport for generations to come.

The Alleged Scheme Unveiled: A Pact for Betrayal

In the wake of the 1919 World Series, whispers of a clandestine agreement circulated within the baseball circles—a pact to intentionally lose the championship games. Eight players, immortalized in infamy as the "Black Sox," including luminaries like "Shoeless" Joe Jackson and Eddie Cicotte, were accused of succumbing to the allure of a ring worth $100,000. The lure of quick riches had seemingly led them down a treacherous path, tarnishing the purity of the game they were entrusted to uphold.

Acquittal and Permanent Banishment: A Paradoxical Verdict

Despite facing allegations of game-fixing, the accused players found themselves in a courtroom drama that would captivate the nation. The legal proceedings resulted in acquittals for the accused, leaving the baseball world in a state of disbelief. However, the apparent triumph of justice was short-lived. Commissioner Kenesaw Mountain Landis, determined to restore the game's integrity, wielded his authority. In a paradoxical twist, the players, though acquitted in a court of law, were permanently banned from Major League Baseball. The gavel of Landis served as the final verdict, severing the ties of these players with the sport they had dishonored.

The Legacy of Infamy: A Bitter Aftertaste

The legacy of the Black Sox Scandal reverberates through the corridors of baseball history, leaving an indelible mark on its collective memory. The stain of betrayal, the betrayal of the game, and the betrayal of the fans lingered long after the accused players left the diamond for the last time. "Shoeless" Joe Jackson, a player of extraordinary talent, became a tragic figure, forever barred from the hallowed halls of the Baseball Hall of Fame.

Reckoning with the Fallout: Reforming the Game

The fallout from the scandal spurred baseball to confront its vulnerabilities and enact sweeping reforms. The appointment of Commissioner Landis heralded a new era of stringent measures aimed at preserving the sport's integrity. The establishment of the office of the Commissioner, endowed with powers to enforce discipline, was a direct response to the Black Sox Scandal. Baseball underwent a metamorphosis, emerging from the shadows of betrayal with a renewed commitment to fair play and the sanctity of competition.

A Cautionary Tale: Lessons for Generations

The Black Sox Scandal stands not only as a cautionary tale but also as a testament to the enduring struggle between the purity of the game and the temptations that threaten its very essence. The banishment of the eight players served as a stark reminder that no individual, regardless of their talent or standing, is above the sanctity of the sport. The scars left by the Black Sox Scandal continue to influence the guardians of baseball, ensuring that the lessons learned from this dark chapter are woven into the very fabric of the game's ethos.

Conclusion: A Haunting Echo in Baseball's Archives

As we conclude our exploration of the Black Sox Scandal, the echoes of betrayal and the lingering bitterness resonate through the annals of baseball's archives. The legacy of the scandal endures as a haunting reminder of the fragility of trust and the relentless pursuit of justice in the face of deception. The stain on the White Sox, the banishment of talented players, and the reforms that followed tell a story of resilience, reform, and an unwavering commitment to safeguarding the spirit of the game. The Black Sox Scandal remains etched in baseball's memory, an enduring testament to the perpetual battle between the hallowed traditions of the sport and the shadows that threaten its very soul.

Chapter 12: A Grand Slam of Popularity: Baseball's Soaring Ascent in the 1920s and 1930s

The 1920s and 1930s witnessed the resounding roar of baseball's ascendance, marking an era where the sport transcended mere competition to become a cultural phenomenon. Chapter 12 unfolds the tale of baseball's rise in popularity, traversing a landscape defined by triumphs, tragedies, and transformative changes.

As the Great War wound down and the nation sought solace, baseball emerged as a beacon of hope and a unifying force. The post-war era was characterized by a collective yearning for normalcy, and baseball, with its timeless rhythm, provided a comforting return to the familiar. The crack of the bat echoed the heartbeat of a nation ready to embrace the joys of the game once more.

The 1920 Season: A Pivotal Moment

As the calendar turned to 1920, baseball found itself at the crossroads of legacy and change. The season, etched in history for various reasons, unfolded with both triumph and tragedy. Notably, it bore witness to the untimely death of Ray Chapman, a talented player of the Cleveland Indians. Struck in the head by a pitch, Chapman succumbed to his injuries a few hours later, becoming the only MLB player to die of an on-field injury. This tragic event cast a solemn shadow over the diamond but also set in motion a series of changes that would shape the future of the game.

Ray Chapman's legacy extended beyond the tragic circumstances of his death. The baseball community mourned the loss of a promising talent, prompting a deep reflection on the safety measures required to protect players. Chapman's memory became a catalyst for reforms aimed at safeguarding the lives of those who took the field, transforming tragedy into a catalyst for positive change.

Chapman's Tragedy and Baseball's Response: A Game in Transition

The death of Ray Chapman sent shockwaves through the baseball community, prompting both reflection and reform. The leagues responded swiftly, recognizing the need for changes to protect players and preserve the essence of the sport. The introduction of new, white baseballs whenever a ball became scuffed or dirty emerged as a safety measure, marking the end of the notorious "dead-ball" era. The game was in transition, evolving to address the challenges posed by its own intensity.

The transition from dark to white baseballs was more than a visual shift—it symbolized a commitment to player safety and an acknowledgment of the game's evolution. This period of transition highlighted baseball's resilience and ability to adapt, reinforcing its status as America's pastime in the face of adversity.

Baseball's Popularity Surges: A Cultural Phenomenon

Amidst triumphs and tribulations, baseball's popularity surged to unprecedented heights. The sport, once confined to the realm of athletics, now blossomed into a cultural phenomenon that captivated the hearts and minds of Americans. The allure of the game transcended demographics, uniting people from all walks of life in a shared passion for the crack of the bat, the roar of the crowd, and the strategic ballet on the diamond.

The surge in popularity wasn't solely due to on-field heroics; it was a cultural shift where baseball became a shared experience. The stadiums were not just venues; they were communal spaces where diverse voices came together in unison, celebrating a sport that mirrored the resilience and diversity of the American spirit.

The End of the Dead-Ball Era: White Baseballs and Renewed Offense

The shift to white baseballs was more than a cosmetic change; it signaled a renaissance in offensive play. The "dead-ball" era, characterized by low-scoring games and a strategic emphasis on small ball, gave way to a new era where hitters could unleash their power with greater freedom. The crackling excitement of home runs echoed through stadiums, transforming the nature of the game and contributing to its newfound popularity.

The adoption of white baseballs didn't just alter aesthetics; it revolutionized the game itself. The renewed emphasis on offense not only thrilled fans but also marked a shift in strategy, with teams now embracing the power of the long ball. Baseball, once a game of meticulous maneuvers, now embraced the exhilaration of the home run.

Cultural Impact: Baseball Beyond the Diamond

Baseball's surge in popularity wasn't confined to the confines of the stadium. It permeated the very fabric of American culture, influencing literature, music, and art. The exploits of baseball legends became legendary tales, woven into the national narrative. The sport became a symbol of resilience, a metaphor for the American spirit in the face of challenges, and a unifying force that bridged divides.

Beyond the diamond, baseball's influence extended to the realms of creativity. Writers penned odes to the crack of the bat, musicians composed ballads of the game's heroes, and artists captured the essence of baseball in brushstrokes. The cultural impact of the sport was not confined to the field; it was a canvas upon which America painted its collective identity.

Emergence of Baseball Heroes: Icons of an Era

The 1920s and 1930s gave rise to a constellation of baseball heroes whose names became synonymous with greatness. From Babe Ruth's towering home runs to Lou Gehrig's enduring fortitude, these players transcended the game, imprinting their legacies on the collective consciousness of a nation. Baseball, once a mere pastime, now had demigods who commanded admiration and adulation.

In the annals of baseball history, the names of Ruth, Gehrig, and their contemporaries weren't just statistics on a scoresheet; they were beacons of inspiration. The emergence of these heroes went beyond their athletic prowess—they became cultural icons, embodying the aspirations and dreams of an entire generation.

Conclusion: Baseball's Golden Age

As we round the bases of this exploration into the rise of baseball's popularity in the 1920s and 1930s, the echoes of history resonate with the cheers of fans and the crack of wooden bats. The tragic loss of Ray Chapman, the transition from the "dead-ball" era, and the emergence of baseball as a cultural force form the tapestry of a golden age. Baseball, with its renewed vigor and cultural impact, stood as more than a sport—it was a reflection of an evolving America, where the roar of the crowd mirrored the pulse of a nation embracing its love for the game. The echoes of this era continue to reverberate, reminding us that baseball's enduring popularity is not just measured in runs and victories but in the indelible imprint it leaves on the soul of a nation.

Chapter 13: The Yankees Dynasty: Roaring Triumphs and Ruthian Feats

In the aftermath of the transformative 1920s and 1930s, a baseball powerhouse emerged to dominate the diamond – the New York Yankees. Chapter 13 delves into the storied legacy of the Yankees, their inaugural World Series appearance, and the remarkable achievements of Babe Ruth, a slugger whose feats transcended the boundaries of the sport.

The Yankees' Inaugural World Series Appearance

The year following the close of the 1920s marked a historic moment in baseball history—the New York Yankees stepped onto the grand stage of the World Series for the first time in 1921. This momentous entry into the pinnacle of baseball showcased the beginning of a dynasty that would leave an indelible mark on the sport.

As the Yankees graced the World Series arena, they brought with them a blend of talent, determination, and a hunger for victory. The storied franchise, born from the consolidation of talent and strategic vision, was destined to redefine the landscape of baseball and etch its name in the annals of greatness.

Yankees' Dominance in the 1930s: A Dynasty Unveiled

The closing chapters of the 1930s bore witness to the emergence of a baseball juggernaut—the New York Yankees. The team's prowess became synonymous with World Series appearances, where they graced the stage of the Fall Classic 11 times. In a staggering display of dominance, the Yankees clinched victory in eight of these World Series, solidifying their status as a dynasty.

The Yankees' ascent to dominance wasn't a mere streak of luck; it was the result of meticulous team-building, strategic foresight, and a commitment to excellence. The Bronx Bombers became more than a team; they became a symbol of baseball supremacy, a force to be reckoned with on the diamond.

Babe Ruth's Ruthless Records: A Slugger's Symphony

At the heart of the Yankees' triumphs stood a colossal figure, both in stature and in the history of baseball – Babe Ruth. The Sultan of Swat left an indelible mark on the record books, rewriting the definition of power hitting. In 1927, Ruth etched his name in history by setting the single-season home run record with an astonishing 60 home runs, a feat that stood as a testament to his unparalleled skill and dominance.

The 1927 season wasn't just a statistical marvel; it was a symphony of power, precision, and unparalleled mastery. Ruth's 60 home runs reverberated through stadiums, capturing the imagination of fans and establishing a benchmark that would stand as a challenge for generations of sluggers to come.

Ruth's Earlier Record: A Glimpse into Greatness

Before the awe-inspiring 1927 season, Babe Ruth had already left an indelible mark on the home run record books. A few years earlier, in 1919, Ruth set the single-season home run record with 29 home runs. This earlier feat showcased Ruth's consistency in reshaping the boundaries of what was deemed possible in the realm of power hitting.

Ruth's earlier record was a precursor to the historic feats that would follow. It signaled the arrival of a baseball titan, a player whose impact on the game was not confined to a single season but reverberated through the years, leaving an everlasting legacy.

Conclusion: The Yankees' Imprint on Baseball History

As Chapter 13 draws to a close, the echoes of the Yankees' inaugural World Series appearance and Babe Ruth's record-breaking heroics linger on the baseball horizon. The emergence of the Yankees as a dominant force and Ruth's unparalleled feats stand as a testament to the enduring spirit of the sport. The dynasty born in the crucible of competition would go on to shape the narrative of baseball in the years to come, leaving an indelible imprint on the pages of history. The Yankees and Babe Ruth had not just played the game; they had become synonymous with the very essence of baseball excellence, forever etching their names into the hallowed halls of the sport's legacy.

Chapter 14: Surviving Hard Times: Baseball in the Grip of the Great Depression

As the 1930s unfolded, a specter of economic hardship cast its shadow over the nation, leaving no corner untouched, including the hallowed grounds of baseball. Chapter 14 navigates the tumultuous landscape as baseball, a symbol of American resilience, grappled with the harsh realities of the Great Depression.

The Great Depression Unfolds: Baseball's Economic Downturn

In the early 1930s, the grip of the Great Depression tightened its hold on America, sending shockwaves through industries, homes, and even the cherished realm of baseball. Afflicted by economic hardship, the national pastime experienced a downturn in popularity, mirroring the struggles faced by millions across the nation. The roaring cheers of the ballpark were muted by the somber echoes of financial uncertainty.

Baseball, once a refuge from the challenges of life, found itself entangled in the broader narrative of economic despair. The iconic status of the sport couldn't shield it from the harsh realities of the Depression, as attendance dwindled and financial woes permeated every aspect of the game.

Financial Woes and Profitability: A Struggling Landscape

By 1932, the financial landscape of Major League Baseball was a stark reflection of the economic turmoil outside the ballpark's walls. Only two MLB teams managed to turn a profit, a staggering decline from more prosperous times. The once-thriving business of baseball faced unprecedented challenges as the nation grappled with the profound economic crisis.

The financial struggles were emblematic of a larger trend—baseball, like many other industries, was not immune to the pervasive impact of the Depression. Franchises that had once flourished now faced the harsh reality of financial insolvency, forcing team owners and executives to navigate uncharted waters.

Attendance Plummets: The Toll of Economic Hardship

As the economic storm raged, attendance at baseball games plummeted. The stands, once filled with fervent fans, now bore witness to empty seats and a palpable sense of austerity. The harsh reality of reduced disposable income, coupled with a 10% federal amusement tax imposed on baseball ticket prices, weighed heavily on the shoulders of fans.

The dwindling attendance painted a poignant picture of the economic toll on the average American. The ballpark, once a communal space for joy and camaraderie, now stood as a testament to the broader struggles faced by individuals and families during this challenging era.

Baseball Adapts: Innovative Strategies for Survival

In the face of adversity, baseball owners and executives demonstrated resilience and innovation. Faced with financial constraints, they implemented strategic measures to ensure the survival of the sport. Rosters were trimmed from 25 men to 23, and even the most esteemed players faced pay cuts. The quest for survival led to the introduction of night games, a revolutionary concept that extended the playing hours and attracted a new audience.

Innovation became the lifeline for baseball. Night games illuminated the diamond under the artificial glow of floodlights, transforming the sport into a spectacle that transcended the confines of daylight. Broadcasting games live by radio further expanded the reach of baseball, bringing the game into the homes of fans who couldn't make it to the ballpark.

Promotions and Women in Baseball: Strategies to Entice Fans

Amid the economic turbulence, baseball executives turned to creative promotions to entice fans back to the ballpark. Free admission for women was one such strategy, a progressive move that aimed to diversify the audience and inject a sense of festivity into the game. These promotional endeavors were not only innovative but also reflective of a concerted effort to adapt to changing societal dynamics.

Baseball, once considered a male-dominated space, opened its doors to women in an unprecedented manner. The free admission promotion not only broadened the demographic appeal of the sport but also signaled a departure from traditional norms.

Resilience Amidst Turmoil: MLB Teams Stand Firm

Throughout the Great Depression, Major League Baseball teams exhibited remarkable resilience. In the face of economic hardship, no MLB teams moved or folded—an extraordinary feat that highlighted the determination of baseball to weather the storm. The sport, woven into the fabric of American culture, stood as a beacon of continuity, offering a sense of normalcy in tumultuous times.

The unwavering commitment of MLB teams to their communities was a testament to the enduring spirit of the sport. As industries crumbled and fortunes waned, baseball remained a constant, providing solace and a sense of continuity amidst the uncertainties of the era.

Conclusion: Baseball's Enduring Legacy

As Chapter 14 concludes, the story of baseball during the Great Depression is one of adaptation, innovation, and resilience. The challenges faced by the sport mirrored the broader struggles of the nation, yet baseball stood as a resilient pillar, weathering the storm and emerging with a renewed sense of purpose. The echoes of this era linger in the annals of baseball history, a testament to the enduring legacy of a sport that transcends the boundaries of time and adversity.

Chapter 15: Baseball's Call to Arms: The Impact of World War II

Chapter 15 unfolds against the backdrop of a world engulfed in the tumult of World War II. As the global conflict reached its crescendo, the impact on baseball was profound, reshaping the composition of teams, altering the narrative of the game, and reflecting the broader societal changes of the era.

The Exodus of Players: A League at War

The onset of World War II marked a seismic shift in the landscape of Major League Baseball. Over 500 players, donning the uniforms of MLB teams, left the diamond to serve their nation in the military. This mass exodus created a void, challenging the continuity of the sport and prompting the emergence of a new era in baseball.

The departure of players for military service echoed the patriotic fervor of the time. Baseball, a cornerstone of American identity, saw its ranks depleted as players traded their gloves for rifles, answering the call to defend freedom on distant fronts.

Service Baseball Teams: A Diamond on the Battlefield

Amidst the chaos of war, baseball remained a source of solace for both soldiers and civilians.

Many departing players found themselves on service baseball teams, entertaining military personnel in the US and across the Pacific. The crack of the bat and the cheers of the crowd became a familiar soundtrack in the most unlikely of places, providing a semblance of normalcy in the midst of global turmoil.

Service baseball teams became a bridge between the war front and home, fostering a sense of camaraderie and nostalgia. The sport's ability to transcend the boundaries of conflict reinforced its status as America's pastime, even in the most challenging of times.

MLB Rosters: A Mosaic of Youth, Experience, and 4F Classifications

The war years transformed the composition of MLB rosters. Teams were now a mosaic of youthful prospects, seasoned veterans, and players classified as 4F—indicating mental, physical, or moral unsuitability for military service. The dynamic shift in team demographics brought a fresh energy to the game, as young talents stepped into roles traditionally held by their departed predecessors.

MLB became a stage for the next generation of ballplayers, each swing and pitch echoing with the aspirations and resilience of a nation grappling with the realities of war. The diamond, once a sanctuary for seasoned professionals, now bore the footprints of those navigating the uncharted waters of wartime baseball.

Pete Gray: Triumph Amidst Adversity

In the tapestry of wartime baseball, one remarkable story stood out—Pete Gray, a one-armed outfielder who defied the odds to advance to the major leagues. Gray's journey encapsulated the spirit of resilience that characterized the era. His presence on the field not only showcased individual triumph but became a symbol of perseverance in the face of adversity.

Gray's story transcended the boundaries of the game, illustrating that in times of challenge, the human spirit has the capacity to overcome physical limitations. His ascent to the major leagues was more than a personal achievement; it was a testament to the indomitable will that defined the wartime generation.

Segregation Persists: MLB's Color Barrier Endures

While the war led to transformative changes in the makeup of MLB teams, one unfortunate constant persisted—the color barrier. Throughout the war, MLB rosters remained devoid of black players. Despite the service and sacrifices of black soldiers, racial segregation persisted in America's pastime, reflecting the deeply entrenched racial prejudices of the time.

The irony of black soldiers fighting for freedom abroad while facing discrimination at home was starkly mirrored in the world of baseball. The exclusion of black players from MLB rosters underscored the deep-rooted racial inequalities that lingered even in the face of global conflict.

Negro League Baseball: A Crucible of Talent and Resilience

While black players were barred from MLB, the war years saw the Negro leagues flourish as a crucible of talent and resilience. Many black players, serving their country in the military, found a haven in Negro league baseball. The stadiums became stages for extraordinary talents, proving that excellence knew no color lines.

The Negro leagues became a testament to the richness of talent that existed beyond the boundaries of MLB. The war years, though marked by segregation, saw the emergence of black baseball legends who would later play pivotal roles in breaking down the color barrier.

Conclusion: The Wartime Tapestry of Baseball

As Chapter 15 draws to a close, the wartime era of baseball emerges as a tapestry woven with sacrifice, triumph, and the enduring spirit of the game. The diamond, though altered by the winds of war, retained its status as a symbol of hope and resilience. From the departure of players for the frontlines to the triumph of one-armed outfielders, baseball mirrored the complexities of a world at war. Yet, the enduring legacy of this era would not only be etched in the record books but also in the hearts of those who found solace and inspiration in the crack of the bat amid the chaos of conflict. The story of World War II and baseball is one of intertwining narratives—a reminder that even in the darkest times, the pursuit of a simple joy on the field could offer a glimmer of normalcy and unity.

Chapter 16: Baseball's Dimmed Lights: Navigating Wartime Blackout Restrictions

Chapter 16 delves into a pivotal period in baseball's history, marked by the shadows of war and the challenges imposed by wartime blackout restrictions. As outdoor lighting was forced to low levels, the very essence of the game, its nighttime contests, faced unprecedented limitations. This chapter explores how baseball grappled with the impact of blackout rules, and the efforts made to keep the sport alive in a world overshadowed by conflict.

Wartime Blackout Restrictions: Dimming the Diamond Lights

Wartime blackout restrictions, designed to mitigate the risk of aerial attacks, cast a literal and metaphorical darkness over baseball. These rules, aimed at keeping outdoor lighting minimal, posed a significant threat to the continuation of night games and extensive travel during the 1942 season. The prospect of a canceled season loomed large, challenging the resilience of the sport during a tumultuous time.

The dimming of the diamond lights not only altered the nocturnal spectacle of baseball but also posed a profound existential question for the sport—how could it endure in an era when the very fabric of daily life was reshaped by the exigencies of war?

Commissioner Landis Pleads for Baseball: A Desperate Appeal

In the face of the looming threat to the 1942 season, MLB Commissioner Kenesaw Mountain Landis took a decisive step. On January 14, 1942, he penned a heartfelt letter to U.S. President Franklin D. Roosevelt, pleading for the continuation of baseball. Landis recognized the power of the sport to uplift the nation's spirit during trying times.

Landis's plea was not merely a defense of baseball; it was an acknowledgment of the role sports play in the collective psyche of a nation. In the crucible of war, he sought to preserve not just a pastime but a source of solace and normalcy.

Roosevelt's Response: Baseball as National Therapy

President Roosevelt's response to Landis's appeal was a resounding affirmation of the importance of baseball during wartime. In a letter that echoed across the pages of history, Roosevelt expressed, "I honestly feel that it would be best for the country to keep baseball going. There will be fewer people unemployed and everybody will work longer hours and harder than ever before. And that means that they ought to have a chance for recreation and for taking their minds off their work even more than before."

Roosevelt's words encapsulated a profound understanding of the human spirit and the vital role recreation plays during times of hardship. Baseball, in his view, was not just a game; it was a form of therapy, a respite for a nation grappling with the weight of war.

Adapting to Darkness: Baseball's Creative Solutions

With Roosevelt's blessing, baseball set out to navigate the challenges posed by blackout restrictions. Creative solutions emerged, as the sport adapted to the constraints of wartime conditions. Strategies such as altered travel schedules and localized blackout exemptions allowed the continuation of night games, albeit with a modified landscape.

Baseball's resilience shone through as it embraced adaptability. The sport, accustomed to the rhythms of summer nights under the floodlights, found a way to persist in the face of external challenges.

Night Games Persist: Illuminating the Spirit

Despite the hurdles, night games persevered during the wartime era. The crack of the bat and the cheers of the crowd reverberated under the muted glow of the lights, offering a semblance of normalcy in a world turned upside down. Baseball, often referred to as America's pastime, became a symbol of continuity—a reminder that even in the darkest hours, the pursuit of joy and camaraderie could endure.

The persistence of night games was not merely a logistical triumph; it was a testament to the indomitable spirit of baseball. In the midst of war-imposed shadows, the diamond lights illuminated not just the playing field but the very soul of the nation.

Conclusion: Shadows Recede, Baseball Prevails

As Chapter 16 concludes, the shadows cast by wartime blackout restrictions begin to recede. Baseball, navigating the challenges with resilience and adaptability, emerges from the darkness. The dimmed lights of the diamond become a metaphor for the indomitable spirit of the sport and its capacity to endure even in the most challenging of times. The echoes of Roosevelt's words linger—a testament to the enduring importance of baseball as a source of recreation, solace, and national therapy during the trials of war.

Chapter 17: Diamonds Amidst Turmoil: Baseball's Resilience During World War II

Chapter 17 unfurls against the backdrop of World War II, a period when the world was gripped by uncertainty, and baseball faced the daunting challenge of maintaining its place in the hearts of a nation on the brink. With the approval of President Franklin D. Roosevelt, the baseball season of 1942 unfolded against a canvas of war, showcasing the sport's resilience and unwavering commitment to providing a semblance of normalcy in tumultuous times.

Spring Training Commences: An Unfazed Beginning

The chapter begins with the approval of President Roosevelt for spring training in 1942. Despite the war raging in distant lands and casting its shadows over American life, the familiar crack of the bat and the rhythmic pop of gloves echoed across ballparks. Spring training, a time of renewal and anticipation, unfolded with a sense of normalcy that belied the global turmoil.

The commencement of spring training symbolized not just the arrival of a new baseball season but a declaration that the game would persist, offering a reprieve for a nation grappling with the challenges of war.

Stars on Hold: Musial, Feller, Williams, DiMaggio

The war, however, was not without its casualties within the realm of baseball. Star players, whose names were synonymous with the sport's greatness, had their careers interrupted. Stan Musial, Bob Feller, Ted Williams, Joe DiMaggio—icons of the diamond—found themselves trading in their baseball uniforms for military attire.

The departure of these stars represented more than just a loss of talent on the field. It was a poignant reminder that the war touched every corner of American life, even its beloved pastime.

Clubs Soldier On: The Indomitable Spirit of Baseball

While stars were called to serve, baseball clubs continued to field their teams. The spirit of competition, the camaraderie in the dugout, and the cheers from the stands persisted. The diamond, though missing some of its brightest gems, remained a stage for the resilience of the game.

Baseball clubs became microcosms of a nation at war, embodying the determination to press on despite adversity. The game, played by those who remained, became a tribute to those who were absent.

The Heartbeat of the Nation: Baseball Endures

As the war interrupted careers and shifted the dynamics of rosters, baseball remained the heartbeat of the nation. The familiar rhythms of the game—the crack of the bat, the roar of the crowd, the strategy of each play—served as a source of comfort and continuity. In ballparks across the country, fans found solace in the enduring spectacle of their beloved pastime.

Baseball endured not just as a game but as a cultural touchstone, a reminder that even in times of upheaval, some constants could be relied upon.

FDR's Approval: Baseball as National Therapy

The approval of President Roosevelt for spring training in 1942 underscored the significance of baseball as a form of national therapy. In the president's words, the continuation of baseball was a means to ensure that people "have a chance for recreation and for taking their minds off their work even more than before." Roosevelt recognized the psychological impact of the game on the collective well-being of a nation at war.

FDR's approval was not merely a nod to the continuation of a sport; it was an acknowledgment of the role baseball played in maintaining the nation's morale during a time of unprecedented challenges.

Conclusion: Baseball's Unyielding Spirit

As Chapter 17 draws to a close, the resilience of baseball during World War II emerges as a testament to the unyielding spirit of the game. The diamond, though transformed by the absence of its brightest stars, continued to shine as a beacon of normalcy and hope. In the face of a global conflict that threatened the very fabric of society, baseball stood firm, proving that even during the darkest of times, the game could endure as a source of joy, camaraderie, and unbroken tradition.

Chapter 18: Breaking Barriers: Jackie Robinson and the Integration of Baseball

Chapter 18 delves into a transformative period in baseball history—one marked by the audacious vision of Branch Rickey, the president and general manager of the Brooklyn Dodgers. In the mid-1940s, Rickey embarked on a mission to challenge the racial segregation that had long defined professional baseball. This chapter explores the groundbreaking efforts to break the color barrier, focusing on the selection of Jackie Robinson, the commitment to integration, and the initiation of what would become known as "The Noble Experiment."

Branch Rickey's Vision: Challenging the Status Quo

At the heart of this chapter is Branch Rickey's unwavering belief in the need to dismantle the racial barriers that pervaded professional baseball. Rickey, a man with a progressive vision, recognized that talent and character knew no racial boundaries. He envisioned a future where players would be judged not by the color of their skin but by the content of their character and their ability on the field.

Rickey's vision was a departure from the norms of an era marked by segregation, and it set the stage for a pivotal moment in the history of baseball.

Selecting Jackie Robinson: A Bold Choice

Rickey's quest for integration led him to a list of promising Negro league players, and among them, he found Jackie Robinson. The selection of Robinson was not merely based on his athletic prowess but also on his character and resilience. Rickey sought not just a skilled player but a trailblazer—a man willing to endure the hardships that breaking the color barrier would inevitably bring.

The choice of Robinson was a bold statement—a declaration that the time for change had come, and the game of baseball would be at the forefront of that change.

The Commitment to Turn the Other Cheek: A Pact with Robinson

Before signing Robinson, Rickey had a crucial conversation with him, extracting a commitment to "turn the other cheek" in the face of racial animosity. This commitment was not just a personal agreement but a strategic move to navigate the storm of racism that awaited Robinson as he stepped onto the field.

Rickey and Robinson forged a pact that went beyond the boundaries of baseball—it was a pact for societal change, one that required immense courage and resilience.

The Noble Experiment Begins: Robinson with the Montreal Royals

In 1946, "The Noble Experiment" commenced as Jackie Robinson, donning the uniform of the Montreal Royals, became the first black baseball player in the International League since the 1880s. This marked the initial phase of Robinson's journey toward breaking the color barrier in Major League Baseball.

The Montreal Royals served as the proving ground for Robinson—a space where he showcased not only his athletic prowess but also the fortitude required to confront the prejudices of the time.

Navigating Adversity: Robinson's Journey

Robinson's presence on the field was met with resistance, hostility, and racial taunts. Yet, true to his commitment, he turned the other cheek. Robinson's journey went beyond baseball; it became a symbol of courage, breaking down not just the color barrier in sports but challenging deeply ingrained societal prejudices.

Robinson's resilience in the face of adversity laid the foundation for the transformative changes that would soon sweep through Major League Baseball.

Conclusion: The Legacy of Integration

As Chapter 18 concludes, the legacy of integration emerges as a defining chapter in baseball history. Branch Rickey's vision and Jackie Robinson's courage paved the way for a more inclusive future. "The Noble Experiment" was not just an experiment—it was a catalyst for change, challenging the ingrained segregation that had marred the sport. The integration of baseball became a microcosm of a broader societal shift, illustrating that the spirit of equality could prevail even in the seemingly impenetrable realms of sports.

The integration of baseball marked a turning point—an acknowledgment that diversity and excellence are not mutually exclusive, but rather, they enrich the fabric of the game and society as a whole.

Chapter 19: The Major League Debut: Jackie Robinson's Triumph at Ebbets Field

Chapter 19 unravels a pivotal moment in baseball history—the major league debut of Jackie Robinson. The culmination of Branch Rickey's vision and Robinson's unwavering commitment, this chapter explores the groundbreaking events of April 15, 1947, when Robinson donned a Brooklyn Dodgers uniform and stepped onto Ebbets Field. It examines the impact of his arrival on the field, the transformative reception from fans, and the reactions within the baseball community.

The Call-Up: Robinson's Ascension to the Majors

In the wake of Robinson's success with the Montreal Royals, the Brooklyn Dodgers decided the time had come to integrate their major league roster. Robinson received the call to join the majors, signaling a seismic shift in the landscape of professional baseball. The anticipation among fans, players, and the nation at large reached a fever pitch as Robinson prepared to make history.

Robinson's call-up was not just an individual achievement; it represented a collective triumph, a step toward dismantling the racial barriers that had long defined the sport.

April 15, 1947: A Date etched in Baseball Lore

On April 15, 1947, a date etched in baseball lore, Jackie Robinson made his major league debut at Ebbets Field. The significance of this moment reverberated far beyond the ballpark's confines. A diverse crowd of 26,623 spectators, including over 14,000 black patrons, gathered to witness history unfold. The atmosphere was electric, charged with the promise of change and the breaking of longstanding racial norms.

Ebbets Field became the stage for a transformation that would resonate through generations—a beacon of hope and progress in the struggle against racial injustice.

The Exodus from Negro Leagues: A Shift in Fandom

Jackie Robinson's entry into the majors triggered a notable shift in the allegiance of black baseball fans. No longer exclusively following Negro league teams, black patrons began flocking to see the Dodgers play, eager to witness Robinson's feats on the diamond. The exodus marked a turning point, as Robinson's presence redefined the dynamics of fandom among black communities.

The departure from Negro league teams was not a rejection but a celebration—a recognition that a new era had dawned, and Robinson's journey was a symbol of hope and empowerment.

Mixed Receptions: Robinson in the Eyes of Media and Players

Robinson's promotion received a generally positive, although mixed, reception. Newspaper writers grappled with the significance of this historic moment, with some embracing the change while others clung to traditional biases. White major league players, too, offered a spectrum of reactions, ranging from supportive to resistant.

The mixed reception mirrored the broader societal struggles around race, highlighting that Robinson's journey was not merely confined to the baseball diamond but intertwined with the complex fabric of American culture.

Manager Durocher's Defiance: A Clear Stand for Inclusion

In the face of the racial tensions surrounding Robinson's entry, Dodgers manager Leo Durocher made a clear and unequivocal stand for inclusion. He famously informed his team, "I don't care if he is yellow or black or has stripes like a zebra. I'm his manager and I say he plays." Durocher's defiance set the tone for the team and sent a powerful message against discrimination.

Durocher's words echoed through the dugout, resonating as a rallying cry for unity and a rebuke to the forces of prejudice.

Conclusion: Jackie Robinson's Impact Beyond the Diamond

As Chapter 19 concludes, the impact of Jackie Robinson's major league debut extends far beyond the boundaries of Ebbets Field. It transcends the realm of sports, becoming a symbol of courage, resilience, and the relentless pursuit of justice. Robinson's journey marked not just a milestone in baseball history but a crucial chapter in the ongoing struggle for civil rights, leaving an indelible legacy that continues to inspire generations.

The major league debut was not just a game-changer for baseball; it was a societal milestone, challenging norms and paving the way for a more inclusive and equitable future.

Chapter 20: Challenges, Triumphs, and a Historic Triumph

Chapter 20 unfolds amidst the threat of a player strike, casting a cloud of uncertainty over baseball. National League President Ford Frick and Baseball Commissioner Happy Chandler's firm stance against striking players intensifies the pressure. In this tumultuous backdrop, Jackie Robinson's resilience becomes a focal point. This chapter explores the challenges Robinson faced during the strike threat, the crucial support from fellow players, and the historic milestone of winning the inaugural Major League Baseball Rookie of the Year Award in a year marked by turmoil.

The Looming Strike Threat: A Crucible for Baseball

The baseball realm is engulfed in turmoil as a strike threat hovers ominously. National League President Ford Frick and Baseball Commissioner Happy Chandler's uncompromising stance sends ripples through the sport. The strike threat emerges as a crucible, testing the mettle of players and the leadership of baseball's governing bodies.

The threat of a strike adds an extra layer of complexity to an already challenging baseball landscape.

Encouragement Amidst Adversity: Robinson's Support Network

Jackie Robinson finds himself at the center of attention, not just for his athletic prowess but for his role as a trailblazer. Despite the looming challenges, Robinson receives significant encouragement from major-league players. Notably, Dodgers teammate Pee Wee Reese emerges as a staunch supporter, emphasizing that color should never be a reason for hatred.

The encouragement Robinson receives becomes a lifeline, reinforcing the collective nature of his groundbreaking journey.

Triumph in Turmoil: Robinson's Rookie of the Year Honor

In the midst of a year marked by uncertainty and challenges, Jackie Robinson achieves a historic milestone by winning the inaugural Major League Baseball Rookie of the Year Award. This accolade not only recognizes Robinson's outstanding performance but also symbolizes a triumph over adversity and underscores his pivotal role in breaking down racial barriers within the sport.

The Rookie of the Year Award stands as a testament to Robinson's resilience and societal impact, a beacon of accomplishment in challenging times.

Unifying Recognition: A Singular Rookie of the Year Honor

It's crucial to note that, in this initial year, separate Rookie of the Year honors for the National League and American League were not awarded until 1949. Robinson's recognition, therefore, stands alone in a league where his presence shattered longstanding norms. The absence of separate awards emphasizes the unique challenges faced by Robinson as he navigated uncharted territory.

Robinson's singular recognition highlights the exceptional nature of his journey and the evolving landscape of acknowledgment for outstanding rookies.

Conclusion: Robinson's Legacy Beyond the Diamond

As Chapter 20 concludes, the enduring legacy of Jackie Robinson comes into focus. From the challenges posed by a strike threat to the encouraging support from peers and the historic achievement of Rookie of the Year, Robinson's journey becomes a testament to resilience, triumph, and the indomitable spirit of a trailblazer.

Robinson's legacy transcends statistics, echoing in the corridors of history as a symbol of courage and societal transformation.

Chapter 21: Expanding Horizons: African-American Pioneers in Major League Baseball

Chapter 21 delves into a transformative period in baseball history, marked by the rapid integration of African-American players into the major leagues. Less than three months after Jackie Robinson's groundbreaking debut, Larry Doby shattered the color barrier in the American League with the Cleveland Indians. This chapter explores the pivotal moments in this era, including the entries of Satchel Paige, Roy Campanella, and Don Newcombe, heralding a new era of diversity in Major League Baseball.

Breaking Barriers: Larry Doby's Entry into the American League

In a testament to the momentum initiated by Jackie Robinson, less than three months later, Larry Doby made history as the first African-American to break the color barrier in the American League. Doby's debut with the Cleveland Indians not only showcased his exceptional talent but further solidified the irreversible shift toward integration within baseball.

The swift succession of African-American pioneers highlights the determination to break down longstanding racial barriers in professional baseball.

A Wave of Talent: The Influx of Black Players

Following Doby's groundbreaking entry, the next year witnessed a surge of African-American players entering the major leagues, contributing to the diversification of the sport. Among the notable signings were pitching legend Satchel Paige by the Indians and the additions of star catcher Roy Campanella and pitcher Don Newcombe by the Dodgers. These signings marked a turning point, demonstrating that talent and skill were the true measures of a player's worth, regardless of their racial background.

The influx of black players symbolizes a shift towards recognizing talent as the primary criterion for entry into the major leagues.

Satchel Paige: A Legend Takes the Stage

The signing of Satchel Paige by the Cleveland Indians adds a new chapter to the history books. Paige, a legendary pitcher from the Negro Leagues, brought his unparalleled skill to the major leagues. His entry not only showcased his extraordinary talent but also highlighted the wealth of untapped potential within the Negro Leagues, enriching the landscape of professional baseball.

Satchel Paige's presence becomes a testament to the wealth of talent in the Negro Leagues and the transformative power of integration.

Roy Campanella and Don Newcombe: Excellence Recognized

The Dodgers, not to be outdone, made significant additions to their roster with the signings of Roy Campanella and Don Newcombe. Campanella, an exceptional catcher, and Newcombe, a formidable pitcher, showcased their prowess on the field. Newcombe's outstanding performance later earned him the distinction of being the first winner of the Cy Young Award, further affirming the success and impact of African-American players in the major leagues.

Campanella and Newcombe's achievements underscore the excellence that transcends racial boundaries in the world of professional baseball.

Conclusion: A Legacy of Diversity Takes Root

As Chapter 21 concludes, the swift succession of African-American players entering the major leagues marks a profound shift in the landscape of baseball. Larry Doby, Satchel Paige, Roy Campanella, and Don Newcombe, among others, become trailblazers in their own right, leaving an indelible mark on the sport. Their contributions set the stage for a legacy of diversity and inclusivity that continues to evolve in Major League Baseball.

The legacy of these pioneers extends beyond the box scores, fostering a more inclusive and diverse future for professional baseball.

Chapter 22: Breaking Down Barriers: Women in Baseball

Chapter 22 delves into the often-overlooked realm of women in baseball, a space historically marked by exclusion and barriers. In 1952, MLB imposed a ban on signing women to contracts, a prohibition that endured for four decades. However, 1992 witnessed a crucial turning point when this ban was finally lifted. This chapter explores the challenges faced by women in their quest for inclusion, the impact of the ban, and the slow but steady progress towards breaking down gender barriers in the world of baseball.

The Ban on Women: MLB's Restriction in 1952

In 1952, Major League Baseball took a regressive step by officially banning the signing of women to contracts. This move, rooted in gender bias and traditional norms, reflected the prevailing societal attitudes of the time. The ban not only limited the opportunities for female players but also sent a discouraging message about the place of women in the world of professional baseball.

The imposition of the ban highlights the deeply ingrained gender stereotypes that permeated the sports landscape in the mid-20th century.

Decades of Exclusion: Women Absent from MLB Rosters

For four decades, the ban on signing women to MLB contracts resulted in a stark absence of female players on major league rosters. The doors of professional baseball remained firmly shut for women, relegating them to the sidelines despite their passion, talent, and potential contributions to the sport. This era of exclusion reflects a broader pattern of gender inequality in sports.

The long period of exclusion underlines the systemic challenges that women faced in their pursuit of equality within the baseball fraternity.

The Long-Awaited Reversal: Ban Lifted in 1992

The turning point finally arrived in 1992 when MLB took a significant stride towards inclusivity by lifting the ban on signing women to contracts. This pivotal moment marked a departure from archaic gender norms and opened the door for women to officially be part of the professional baseball landscape. The decision to lift the ban was not just a policy shift; it symbolized a recognition of the evolving role of women in sports.

The lifting of the ban represents a triumph for advocates of gender equality and a recognition of the changing dynamics within the world of baseball.

The Absence Persists: No Female MLB Players Yet

Despite the ban being lifted, the stark reality remains that, as of now, there have been no female players in Major League Baseball. While progress has been made in breaking down some barriers, challenges persist in terms of creating a pathway for women to compete at the highest level. The absence of female MLB players prompts reflection on the continued work required to achieve true gender equity in baseball.

The absence of female players at the highest level underscores the need for continued efforts to bridge the gender gap in professional baseball.

Conclusion: Navigating Toward Equality

As Chapter 22 concludes, the journey of women in baseball reflects both progress and persistent challenges. From the imposition of a ban to its eventual lifting, the narrative evolves, offering hope for a more inclusive future. Yet, the absence of female players in MLB emphasizes the ongoing work needed to fully realize gender equality in the realm of baseball.

The chapter closes with the acknowledgment that while strides have been made, the pursuit of equality for women in baseball is an ongoing and essential journey.

Chapter 23: Shifting Landscapes: Relocation and Expansion in Major League Baseball

Chapter 23 unfolds against the backdrop of a baseball landscape marked by stability and regional concentration. From 1903 to 1953, Major League Baseball comprised two eight-team leagues, with 16 teams scattered across ten cities in the northeastern and midwestern United States. New York City boasted three teams, while Boston, Chicago, Philadelphia, and St. Louis each housed two. However, this era of equilibrium faced transformative shifts starting in the 1950s. This chapter explores the dynamics of team relocation and the expansion of Major League Baseball, unraveling a narrative of change and adaptation.

Era of Stability: Two Leagues, Ten Cities

For half a century, from 1903 to 1953, Major League Baseball embraced a stable structure. The major leagues, consisting of the American League and the National League, featured two eight-team leagues. The 16 teams were strategically located in ten cities, primarily concentrated in the northeastern and midwestern regions of the United States. This period of stability, although geographically limited, laid the foundation for a sport that captured the imagination of fans across the nation.

The structure of two leagues in ten cities becomes synonymous with an era of baseball marked by regional concentration and stability.

Geographic Constraints: The Limitations of Team Locations

The geography of Major League Baseball during this era posed inherent challenges. New York City emerged as a baseball hub with three teams, while other cities like Boston, Chicago, Philadelphia, and St. Louis accommodated two teams each. St. Louis, positioned as the southernmost and westernmost city with a major league team, represented the outer limits of the baseball map. The extensive travel required for the longest road trip, from Boston to St. Louis, vividly underscores the geographic constraints of the time, with a 24-hour journey by railroad.

The geographic limitations of team locations set the stage for future shifts as baseball's landscape continued to evolve.

A Turning Point: Teams on the Move (1953-1955)

The 1950s heralded a new era of change as teams, previously anchored in cities with multiple teams, embarked on a journey to uncharted territories. Between 1953 and 1955, three teams initiated this transformative trend by relocating to new cities.

The Boston Braves became the Milwaukee Braves, the St. Louis Browns transformed into the Baltimore Orioles, and the Philadelphia Athletics undertook a shift to become the Kansas City Athletics. This period marked the beginning of a significant departure from the longstanding stability that characterized the preceding decades.

The relocation of three teams signifies a departure from tradition, setting the stage for a dynamic era of movement and expansion.

Expansion and Adaptation: A Shifting Baseball Landscape

The latter part of the 1950s saw the initiation of a broader trend: the expansion of Major League Baseball. Teams moved beyond the confines of cities with established baseball traditions, venturing into unexplored territories. This expansion not only reshaped the geographical footprint of the sport but also paved the way for the emergence of new fan bases and regional rivalries. Baseball's landscape, once characterized by stability, now stood on the cusp of a transformative journey.

The expansion of MLB introduces a new chapter, reflecting the adaptability of the sport to changing demographics and fan interests.

Conclusion: The Ever-Changing Tapestry of Baseball

As Chapter 23 draws to a close, the narrative of relocation and expansion emerges as a crucial chapter in the story of Major League Baseball. The stability of two leagues and ten cities gives way to a dynamic era where teams embrace new horizons. The ever-changing tapestry of baseball, woven through shifts in geography and the pursuit of wider audiences, reflects the sport's ability to evolve and captivate generations of fans.

The chapter concludes with the understanding that the essence of baseball lies not only in the game itself but in the ever-shifting narrative of its teams and the communities they call home.

Chapter 24: The Westward Shift: Baseball's Expansion to the Coast

Chapter 24 unfolds against the backdrop of the 1958 Major League Baseball season, a pivotal period that transformed the landscape of the sport and paved the way for its nationwide reach. At the center of this transformative season was Walter O'Malley, the influential owner of the Brooklyn Dodgers, whose bold decision to move the team to Los Angeles marked a historic shift. This chapter explores the dynamics of this Westward expansion, the persuasive maneuvers that brought the rival New York Giants to San Francisco, and the ripple effects that turned Major League Baseball into a truly national league.

Walter O'Malley's Influence: The Architect of Change

Walter O'Malley, often regarded as the most influential owner of baseball's early expansion era, emerges as a central figure in the narrative of the 1958 season. O'Malley's vision extended beyond the traditional confines of the sport, and his decision to move the Brooklyn Dodgers to Los Angeles set in motion a chain of events that would reshape Major League Baseball. O'Malley's influence extended not only to the Dodgers but also to the rival New York Giants, marking the beginning of a Westward shift.

O'Malley's bold vision and decisive actions set the stage for a new era of baseball that transcended geographical boundaries.

The Westward Exodus: Dodgers to Los Angeles

In a historic move, Walter O'Malley orchestrated the relocation of the Brooklyn Dodgers to Los Angeles, marking the first major league franchise on the West Coast. This monumental decision not only altered the geographic footprint of Major League Baseball but also opened up new horizons for the sport's expansion. The Dodgers' move to the West Coast was a pioneering venture that would prove to be a catalyst for future relocations and the broader nationalization of the league.

The Dodgers' relocation to Los Angeles symbolizes the beginning of a transformative period in baseball history.

Persuading the Giants: San Francisco Beckons

Walter O'Malley's influence extended beyond the Dodgers when he successfully persuaded the New York Giants to move west and become the San Francisco Giants. The persuasive maneuvers unfolded amid considerations by Giants owner Horace Stoneham to relocate to Minnesota due to declining attendance at the Polo Grounds.

O'Malley's invitation for Stoneham to meet San Francisco Mayor George Christopher in New York proved instrumental in sealing the deal. The joint move of the Dodgers and the Giants to the West Coast marked a strategic alignment that would prove beneficial for both franchises and Major League Baseball as a whole.

The successful persuasion of the Giants to move to San Francisco cements the Westward shift as a collaborative effort with far-reaching implications.

Commissioner Frick's Resistance and Success of the Dual Move

MLB Commissioner Ford Frick initially opposed the meeting between O'Malley and Stoneham, reflecting the resistance to the idea of relocating two storied franchises simultaneously. However, the dual moves proved to be a resounding success for both the Dodgers and the Giants, as well as for Major League Baseball. The economic viability of West Coast road trips for visiting teams and the surge in attendance, exemplified by the Dodgers setting a single-game MLB attendance record in their first home appearance, underscored the success of this Westward expansion.

The resistance from Commissioner Frick gives way to the undeniable success of the dual move, showcasing the foresight of O'Malley and the positive impact on the league.

Conclusion: A New Horizon for Baseball

As Chapter 24 concludes, the Westward shift initiated by Walter O'Malley's bold decisions ushers in a new era for Major League Baseball. The relocation of the Dodgers and the Giants to the West Coast not only expands the geographic footprint of the sport but also sets the stage for baseball's evolution into a truly nationwide league. The resonance of this transformative season reverberates through the record-breaking attendance, economic viability, and the establishment of a precedent for future franchise relocations.

The chapter closes with the recognition that the 1958 season marks a turning point, propelling baseball toward a horizon of broader possibilities and national prominence.

Chapter 25: Expansion and Evolution: The 1960s Reshape Major League Baseball

Chapter 25 delves into the 1960s, a pivotal decade that witnessed significant changes in Major League Baseball's landscape. The era was marked by franchise relocations, the addition of new teams, and the emergence of notable clubs that would go on to shape the narrative of the sport. In 1961, a seismic shift occurred as the Washington Senators moved to Minneapolis–St. Paul, becoming the Minnesota Twins. Simultaneously, the American and National Leagues expanded with the inclusion of the Los Angeles Angels, a new Washington Senators franchise, the Houston Astros, and the New York Mets. This chapter explores the impact of these changes on the league's dynamics and the notable achievements of the expansion teams.

The Minnesota Twins: A New Identity in the Heartland

The relocation of the first Washington Senators franchise to Minneapolis–St. Paul in 1961 marked the birth of the Minnesota Twins. This move not only introduced a new geographic identity for the team but also reflected the changing demographic and cultural landscape of Major League Baseball. The Twins, now situated in the heartland, would go on to establish themselves as a competitive force in the American League.

The birth of the Minnesota Twins symbolizes the league's adaptability to shifting demographics and its commitment to embracing new regions.

The American League Expansion: Angels in Anaheim and a Reborn Senators

The same year witnessed the addition of two new teams to the American League—the Los Angeles Angels and a fresh Washington Senators franchise. The Angels, initially located in downtown L.A. before moving to nearby Anaheim, added a West Coast flair to the league. The reimagined Washington Senators, although a continuation of the original franchise, embarked on a new chapter, contributing to the evolving narrative of baseball in the nation's capital.

The American League expansion introduces new teams and injects fresh energy into the league's competitive landscape.

National League Expansion: Astros and Mets Enter the Scene

In 1962, the National League expanded with the inclusion of the Houston Astros and the New York Mets. The Astros, initially known as the "Colt .45s," made history by becoming the first southern major league franchise since the Louisville Colonels in 1899. Positioned along the Gulf Coast, the Astros brought a unique regional flavor to the league.

Meanwhile, the Mets, based in the nation's media capital, faced early struggles, but their journey would ultimately culminate in a remarkable turnaround.

The addition of the Astros and Mets broadens the geographical reach of the National League and sets the stage for diverse baseball narratives.

Mets' Miracle: From Futility to World Series Triumph

The New York Mets quickly gained a reputation for futility, going 40–120 in their inaugural season. However, their narrative took an unexpected turn in their eighth season (1969) when they became the first of the 1960s expansion teams to reach the postseason. Against the heavily favored Baltimore Orioles, the Mets secured a stunning World Series title, solidifying their place in baseball history and inspiring a generation of fans with their improbable triumph.

The Mets' journey from futility to World Series glory becomes a defining story of resilience and the unpredictable nature of baseball.

Conclusion: A Decade Redefined

Chapter 25 draws to a close, encapsulating a transformative decade that reshaped Major League Baseball. The 1960s witnessed a shift in geographic identities, the inclusion of new teams, and the rise of unexpected contenders. The league's ability to adapt to these changes not only diversified its fanbase but also set the stage for a future where baseball's reach would extend far beyond its traditional strongholds.

The chapter concludes by recognizing the 1960s as a decade that laid the foundation for a dynamic and evolving Major League Baseball.

Chapter 26: New Frontiers: Expanding Horizons in the Late 1960s

Chapter 26 navigates through the late 1960s, a period characterized by bold moves and expansions that altered the geographical footprint of Major League Baseball. In 1966, the major leagues ventured into the "Deep South" with the relocation of the Braves to Atlanta. The following years witnessed further shifts, with the Kansas City Athletics moving to Oakland in 1968 and both the American and National Leagues welcoming new expansion franchises in 1969. This chapter explores the impact of these transformative events, marking a significant chapter in the league's evolution.

The Braves' Southern Odyssey: Atlanta Beckons

In 1966, Major League Baseball made a historic move to the "Deep South" as the Braves relocated from Milwaukee to Atlanta. This shift not only introduced a major league presence to the city but also marked a pivotal moment in the league's efforts to expand its reach into previously untapped regions. The Braves' move to Atlanta set the stage for the emergence of the South as a significant baseball hub.

The Braves' relocation to Atlanta signifies the league's commitment to expanding its presence into new territories.

Westward Bound: Athletics Find a Home in Oakland

The West Coast continued to emerge as a baseball stronghold when the Kansas City Athletics migrated westward to become the Oakland Athletics in 1968. This move not only solidified the West Coast's position in Major League Baseball but also contributed to the formation of a fierce baseball rivalry with the San Francisco Giants. The Athletics' relocation added a new dimension to the league's dynamics, further emphasizing the nationalization of baseball.

The Athletics' move to Oakland strengthens the league's foothold on the West Coast, setting the stage for iconic rivalries.

Expansion Fever: Welcoming New Franchises

The year 1969 marked a significant expansion for both the American and National Leagues, with each adding two new franchises. The American League welcomed the Seattle Pilots and the Kansas City Royals, while the National League expanded into Canada with the introduction of the Montreal Expos and added the San Diego Padres to its roster. This expansion not only broadened the league's geographical scope but also paved the way for a more diverse and inclusive Major League Baseball.

The addition of new franchises reflects the league's commitment to embracing expansion and fostering diversity.

Seattle Pilots to Milwaukee Brewers: A Brief Yet Impactful Stint

The Seattle Pilots, one of the expansion teams added in 1969, faced challenges that led to their relocation after just one season. The team moved to Milwaukee and underwent a transformation, emerging as the Milwaukee Brewers. Despite their brief tenure in Seattle, the Pilots left an indelible mark on the league, highlighting the unpredictable nature of franchise trajectories.

The Seattle Pilots' journey to becoming the Milwaukee Brewers exemplifies the resilience and adaptability of Major League Baseball.

The Canadian Connection: Montreal Expos Make History

In a historic move, the National League welcomed its first Canadian franchise—the Montreal Expos—in 1969. This marked a significant moment in baseball history, signaling the league's global expansion and underscoring its ability to transcend national borders. The Expos became a symbol of baseball's international reach, paving the way for future cross-border collaborations.

The Montreal Expos' entry into the National League represents a groundbreaking step in the globalization of Major League Baseball.

Conclusion: A Decade of Expansion and Transformation

As Chapter 26 concludes, the late 1960s stand as a decade of expansion and transformation for Major League Baseball. The league's foray into the "Deep South," the establishment of a West Coast rivalry, and the addition of new franchises underscore a commitment to adaptability and growth. The expansion of the league's footprint and the introduction of teams from diverse regions lay the groundwork for a future where baseball's influence would extend far beyond its traditional boundaries.

The chapter closes with an acknowledgment of the late 1960s as a period that not only redefined the league's geography but also set the stage for a more expansive and globally connected Major League Baseball.

Chapter 27: Shifting Landscapes: Baseball's Expanding Borders in the 1970s

Chapter 27 delves into the dynamic landscape of Major League Baseball during the 1970s, marked by significant relocations and the addition of new franchises. In 1972, the second iteration of the Washington Senators relocated to the Dallas–Fort Worth metroplex, transforming into the Texas Rangers. The expansion continued in 1977 with the introduction of the Toronto Blue Jays and the Seattle Mariners. This chapter explores the motivations behind these moves and their impact on the league's narrative.

The Texas Two-Step: Senators Become Rangers

In 1972, the Washington Senators embarked on a journey to the Dallas–Fort Worth metroplex, undergoing a transformative shift that would see them emerge as the Texas Rangers. The move to Texas not only reflected the league's openness to exploring new markets but also signaled the growing influence of baseball in the southern United States.

The relocation of the Senators to Texas adds a Southern flavor to the league, showcasing baseball's expanding appeal.

Blue Jays Soar: Baseball's Northern Expansion

In 1977, Major League Baseball extended its reach into Canada once again, adding the Toronto Blue Jays to its roster of teams. This move not only emphasized the league's commitment to international expansion but also marked the Blue Jays as trailblazers in Canadian baseball. The introduction of a second Canadian team highlighted baseball's growing popularity beyond the traditional American boundaries.

The inclusion of the Toronto Blue Jays underscores baseball's global vision and its ability to transcend national borders.

Mariners Set Sail: The Emergence of Seattle

The same expansion in 1977 saw the birth of the Seattle Mariners, bringing Major League Baseball to the Pacific Northwest. The Mariners' entry into the league not only added another West Coast team but also laid the foundation for a passionate baseball culture in Seattle. This move reflected the league's strategic expansion into untapped regions, further solidifying its presence on the West Coast.

The arrival of the Mariners in Seattle expands the league's footprint, tapping into the vibrant baseball culture of the Pacific Northwest.

A Decade of Stability: The 1990s and Beyond

Following the flurry of relocations and expansions in the 1970s, Major League Baseball experienced a period of stability, with no new teams added until the 1990s. This era of relative consistency allowed existing franchises to establish themselves in their respective markets, fostering a sense of continuity and tradition within the league.

The 1990s mark a period of stability, allowing existing teams to solidify their presence and deepen their connections with local communities.

The Dormant Years: No Teams on the Move

From 1977 until 2005, no teams underwent relocation, contributing to a sense of stability within the league. This dormant period allowed franchises to build enduring relationships with their fan bases and communities, reinforcing the idea that baseball had become an integral part of the cultural fabric in various regions.

The absence of team relocations for nearly three decades fosters a sense of continuity and permanence within Major League Baseball.

Conclusion: A Chapter of Growth and Stability

As Chapter 27 draws to a close, the 1970s stand out as a transformative decade in Major League Baseball. The relocation of the Senators to Texas, the addition of the Blue Jays and Mariners, and the subsequent years of stability reflect a league in constant evolution. These developments set the stage for the continued expansion and globalization of baseball, laying the foundation for a future where the sport's influence would extend even further beyond its traditional borders.

The chapter concludes by highlighting the 1970s as a pivotal era that shaped the modern landscape of Major League Baseball, showcasing a delicate balance between growth and stability.

Chapter 28: The Pitcher's Renaissance: Dominance and Rule Changes

Chapter 28 delves into a pivotal era in baseball, the late 1960s, where the balance between pitchers and hitters underwent a dramatic shift. Dubbed "the year of the pitcher," 1968 witnessed unprecedented feats on the mound, challenging hitters and prompting rule changes that would shape the game's future. This chapter explores the dominance of pitchers and the rule alterations that ensued.

The Pitcher's Triumph: Yastrzemski, McLain, and Gibson

In the memorable year of 1968, Carl Yastrzemski of the Boston Red Sox claimed the American League batting title with a modest .301 average, marking the lowest in the history of Major League Baseball. Meanwhile, Denny McLain, the ace pitcher for the Detroit Tigers, achieved a remarkable feat by winning 31 games in a single season, a feat unparalleled since Dizzy Dean's 1934 season. St. Louis Cardinals' Bob Gibson further solidified the pitcher's reign by posting an extraordinary 1.12 ERA.

The 1968 season witnessed unparalleled performances by Yastrzemski, McLain, and Gibson, showcasing the dominance of pitchers on both ends of the league.

The Year of the Pitcher: A Statistical Anomaly

1968's statistical anomalies prompted a reassessment of the game's dynamics. The unprecedented success of pitchers raised questions about the viability of hitting strategies and led to an exploration of factors contributing to this extraordinary pitching prowess.

The statistical anomalies of 1968 provoke a reevaluation of baseball strategies and prompt discussions on the evolving dynamics between pitchers and hitters.

The Pitcher-Friendly Rules: Lowering the Mound and Shrinking the Strike Zone

In response to the overwhelming dominance of pitchers, Major League Baseball implemented rule changes aimed at leveling the playing field. The lowering of the pitcher's mound and adjustments to the strike zone were pivotal in restoring equilibrium between offense and defense.

Rule changes, including lowering the mound and adjusting the strike zone, aimed at restoring balance between pitchers and hitters.

Aftermath: The Impact on Baseball Strategy and Tactics

The alterations in rules not only transformed the statistical landscape but also had a profound impact on how teams approached the game strategically. Managers and players adapted to the new conditions, leading to shifts in offensive and defensive tactics.

The rule changes of the late 1960s prompted a strategic reevaluation, influencing how teams approached both offensive and defensive aspects of the game.

Legacy: Pitching Dominance in Perspective

As Chapter 28 concludes, it reflects on the enduring legacy of the pitcher's dominance in the late 1960s. While the rule changes aimed to restore balance, they left an indelible mark on the game, influencing pitching strategies and shaping the dynamics between pitchers and hitters for years to come.

The legacy of pitching dominance, shaped by the events of the late 1960s, continues to influence the game's dynamics and strategies in the contemporary era.

Chapter 29: A New Horizon: Rule Changes Reshape the Game

In the annals of baseball history, 1968 stands out as the "Year of the Pitcher." The dominance displayed by hurlers like Denny McLain and Bob Gibson raised eyebrows and prompted a reevaluation of the sport's equilibrium. Chapter 29 explores the pivotal decisions made by the MLB Playing Rules Committee in response to the lopsided pitcher-hitter dynamic, ushering in an era of transformative rule changes that would redefine the very essence of the game.

The Committee's Decision: Addressing the Pitcher's Dominance

Faced with a pressing need for action, the MLB Playing Rules Committee convened in December 1968 to deliberate on the unprecedented dominance of pitchers. The statistics from the 1968 season were staggering, with pitchers holding a distinct advantage. The committee, comprised of baseball luminaries and experts, recognized the urgency of restoring balance and fairness to the game.

The pivotal decision to redefine the strike zone and lower the pitcher's mound reflected a commitment to preserving the integrity of baseball. The committee understood that a game characterized by overwhelming pitching superiority risked alienating fans and stifling the excitement inherent in the sport.

Redrawing the Strike Zone: From Shoulders to Armpits

A central component of the committee's strategy involved a radical redefinition of the strike zone. The previous parameters, spanning from knees to shoulders, were perceived as tipping the scales too heavily in favor of pitchers. The new strike zone, from the top of the knees to the armpits, aimed to level the playing field by providing hitters with a more reasonable chance to connect with pitches.

The significance of this alteration extended beyond numerical metrics; it was a philosophical shift that sought to rejuvenate the offensive dynamics of baseball. By expanding the strike zone vertically, the committee aspired to rekindle the exhilaration of high-scoring games and the thrill of well-contested at-bats.

Lowering the Mound: Leveling the Playing Field

Recognizing the pivotal role of the pitcher's mound in dictating the outcome of games, the committee opted to address this aspect as well. The decision to lower the pitcher's mound from 15 to 10 inches aimed to diminish the physical advantage pitchers enjoyed. By altering the trajectory of pitches, it was anticipated that hitters would have an improved chance of making contact and driving the offensive narrative of the game.

This adjustment wasn't merely a pragmatic response to statistical anomalies but a nuanced understanding of the symbiotic relationship between the pitcher's mound and the ebb and flow of baseball. It was a strategic move that sought to recalibrate the delicate equilibrium between offense and defense.

Immediate Impact: The 1969 Season Unfolds

As the 1969 season dawned, the baseball world held its breath in anticipation of the effects of these sweeping changes. Teams, managers, and players grappled with the task of adapting to the new strike zone and the altered pitcher's mound height. The adjustments were palpable, giving rise to a season characterized by transition and experimentation.

The immediate impact of the rule changes was visible in the statistical shifts and the evolution of gameplay strategies. Teams reevaluated their approach to pitching and hitting, and players honed new skills to align with the transformed dynamics of the sport.

Reception and Critique: Mixed Responses to Change

The implementation of these groundbreaking changes elicited a spectrum of responses within the baseball community. While some welcomed the adjustments as a necessary corrective measure, others voiced concerns about the departure from tradition and the potential erosion of the sport's core essence.

The mixed reactions underscored the inherent tension between tradition and progress, a perennial debate that accompanies any substantial alteration to the fabric of baseball. As fans and players grappled with the ramifications, the 1969 season became a crucible for evaluating the success of the committee's intervention.

Long-Term Effects: Shaping the Modern Game

Chapter 29 concludes by casting a retrospective gaze on the enduring legacy of the rule changes of 1969. Beyond the immediate impact on that season, these adjustments laid the foundation for the modern game. The recalibration of the strike zone and pitcher's mound contributed to a more dynamic, balanced, and fan-friendly version of baseball that continues to captivate audiences to this day.

The enduring effects of the rule changes underscore the capacity of baseball to evolve while staying true to its timeless essence. As subsequent chapters will reveal, the decisions made in 1969 set in motion a trajectory that would shape the sport for generations to come.

Chapter 30: The DH Dilemma: Revolutionizing Offense in the American League

The early 1970s marked a pivotal period in baseball, characterized by an earnest desire to rejuvenate the offensive dimensions of the game. Chapter 30 delves into the inception and impact of the designated hitter (DH) rule, a groundbreaking initiative undertaken by the American League in 1973. This rule, born out of a quest for higher scoring and increased fan engagement, would go on to reshape the dynamics of baseball and spark enduring debates within the baseball community.

The Genesis of the Designated Hitter: An Offensive Experiment

As the American League grappled with attendance disparities compared to its National League counterpart, league executives and baseball authorities sought innovative measures to inject excitement into the game. The idea of introducing a designated hitter—a player designated solely for batting, without the requirement to play a defensive position—emerged as a daring experiment to tip the balance in favor of offense.

In 1973, the American League implemented the DH rule, allowing teams to incorporate a power hitter into their lineup without compromising defensive prowess. The move was met with anticipation and skepticism, as traditionalists questioned the departure from the longstanding tradition of pitchers batting.

The DH in Action: Offense Takes Center Stage

The immediate impact of the designated hitter was palpable. Teams now had the luxury of fielding a potent offensive player without worrying about defensive liabilities. This shift was particularly evident in the increased frequency of home runs, a surge in batting averages, and a rise in run production. The DH rule succeeded in its primary objective—making games more thrilling for fans and enhancing the overall entertainment value of baseball.

Players like Frank Thomas, David Ortiz, and Edgar Martinez became synonymous with the designated hitter role, showcasing the strategic advantage it afforded teams. The DH not only extended the careers of aging sluggers but also provided managers with a tactical tool to navigate critical moments in games.

The DH Debate: Tradition vs. Innovation

While the DH rule undeniably injected a newfound vigor into American League lineups, it also ignited fervent debates within the baseball community. Traditionalists lamented the departure from a century-old practice of pitchers batting, arguing that it undermined the holistic nature of the game. The essence of baseball, they contended, lay in the dual responsibility of players to contribute both offensively and defensively.

Conversely, proponents of the DH extolled its virtues in diversifying strategies and intensifying the spectacle for fans. The DH became a symbol of baseball's adaptability to the evolving tastes and expectations of a broadening audience.

The DH Spreads: Interleague Play and Beyond

Initially confined to the American League, the DH rule's success and popularity prompted discussions about its potential expansion. In 1997, with the introduction of interleague play, National League teams faced the DH in games played in American League parks, further blurring the lines between the two leagues. This cross-league experimentation added a layer of intrigue to matchups and intensified the ongoing debate about the DH's place in the broader landscape of baseball.

Legacy of the DH: A Permanent Fixture and Ongoing Debate

As the years unfolded, the designated hitter entrenched itself as a permanent fixture in the American League, contributing to the evolution of offensive strategies and player roles. The DH rule, however, remained a point of contention whenever discussions arose about uniformity between the two leagues.

Chapter 30 concludes by examining the lasting legacy of the DH rule and its enduring impact on the game. Whether viewed as a symbol of innovation or a departure from tradition, the designated hitter has left an indelible mark on baseball, shaping the sport's trajectory in unforeseen ways. The ongoing debate surrounding the DH continues to reflect the delicate balance between honoring baseball's rich heritage and embracing the winds of change that sweep through America's pastime.

Chapter 31: The New Ballgame - Innovations and Challenges in Baseball

As baseball entered the 1970s, a wave of innovation and adaptation swept through the sport. This chapter explores the introduction of the designated hitter (DH) rule in the American League, a move aimed at increasing scoring and reshaping the dynamics of the game. Additionally, the era witnessed the rise of artificial turf and the construction of multi-purpose stadiums, altering the playing field and challenging traditional norms.

The 1970s marked a period of experimentation and adjustment as Major League Baseball (MLB) sought to enhance the fan experience, accommodate new trends, and address the evolving expectations of a growing audience. The landscape of baseball was changing, presenting both opportunities and challenges.

The Designated Hitter: A Radical Shift

In 1973, the American League introduced the designated hitter (DH) rule, a departure from the traditional structure where pitchers took their turn at bat. The DH, a position player designated to bat in place of the pitcher, aimed to inject more offense into the game. This rule change, however, sparked debates about the integrity of the sport and the impact on strategy.

The introduction of the DH was met with mixed reactions from players, managers, and fans. Traditionalists lamented the alteration of a fundamental aspect of baseball strategy, while proponents argued that the change would make the game more exciting for a broader audience. The DH rule would come to symbolize the ongoing tension between tradition and innovation in the sport.

Artificial Turf: A Synthetic Revolution

Synthetic playing surfaces made from artificial turf gained popularity in the 1970s, especially in multi-purpose stadiums. The appeal of artificial turf lay in its durability, low maintenance, and adaptability to various weather conditions. However, players soon discovered that the unforgiving surface came with its own set of challenges, influencing playing styles and redefining defensive strategies.

The adoption of artificial turf raised questions about the toll on players' bodies and the overall quality of the game. The increased speed of play and unique bounces off the synthetic surface demanded adjustments, leading to an era where teams prioritized speed and defensive prowess. Baseball was evolving not only in strategy but also in the very nature of gameplay.

Changing Dynamics: Speed and Defense

The shift to artificial turf and the DH rule altered the dynamics of baseball fundamentally. With the emphasis on speed and defensive skills, teams sought players who could cover ground efficiently, turning stolen bases and strategic baserunning into valuable assets. The game, once dominated by power hitting, now embraced a more nuanced approach that valued agility and quick thinking.

Players adapted to the changing landscape, recognizing that success on the field required a multifaceted skill set. Speedsters became prized assets, and teams reevaluated their rosters to align with the new demands of the game. The 1970s marked a period of transition, as baseball sought to find a balance between tradition and the evolving tastes of a modern audience.

Stadium Aesthetics: The Multi-Purpose Trend

The 1970s witnessed a surge in the construction of multi-purpose stadiums, designed to host both baseball and football games. These venues, such as Three Rivers Stadium in Pittsburgh and Veterans Stadium in Philadelphia, became emblematic of an era that prioritized economic efficiency and versatility. However, the circular designs and artificial turf surfaces also brought about a departure from the traditional aesthetics of baseball.

As the landscape of baseball stadiums transformed, so did the visual experience for fans. The circular designs, while efficient for hosting multiple sports, challenged the iconic imagery of the baseball diamond. The juxtaposition of tradition and innovation was evident in the architectural evolution of baseball stadiums.

Criticisms and Challenges: The Human Element

While innovations like the DH rule and artificial turf promised benefits for the sport, concerns emerged about their impact on players' well-being. The toll on players' bodies, coupled with debates about the aesthetic and strategic implications of these changes, highlighted the delicate balance between progress and preserving the essence of baseball.

As players grappled with the physical challenges posed by artificial turf, and traditionalists questioned the soul of the game with the introduction of the DH, baseball found itself at a crossroads. The human element became a focal point in discussions about the direction the sport was heading, prompting a broader reflection on the evolving identity of baseball.

Conclusion: A Period of Evolution and Controversy

The 1970s unfolded as a dynamic and controversial chapter in the history of baseball. From the radical introduction of the designated hitter to the widespread adoption of artificial turf and the construction of multi-purpose stadiums, the sport navigated uncharted territory. As baseball embraced innovation, it grappled with the tensions between tradition and progress. The legacy of this era would linger, shaping the future trajectory of the game and laying the groundwork for further transformations in the decades to come.

Chapter 32: The Evolution of Strategy - Pitching, Speed, and Changing Dynamics

The 1980s witnessed a profound transformation in the strategies employed by baseball teams. From a focus on pitching prowess to the rise of speed on the basepaths, this chapter delves into the changing dynamics that shaped the game. As teams adapted to the nuances of artificial surfaces and embraced a new philosophy regarding starting pitchers, baseball underwent a strategic renaissance.

The shifting landscape of baseball in the 1980s was marked by a departure from traditional norms. Teams began to reevaluate their approach to pitching, emphasizing the importance of bullpens, and sought ways to exploit the advantages provided by artificial surfaces. The era witnessed a recalibration of offensive and defensive strategies, giving rise to a new era of baseball dynamics.

Building Around Pitching: The Bullpen Revolution

In the 1980s, teams recognized the strategic importance of building their rosters around a strong bullpen. As artificial surfaces altered the game's dynamics, the ability to deploy effective relievers became a key factor in a team's success. Managers increasingly relied on setup men and closers to secure victories, shifting away from the traditional expectation of starting pitchers completing games.

The evolution of the bullpen marked a departure from the era of complete-game dominance. Teams invested in developing deep and reliable relief pitching staffs, allowing them to maintain control and strategically manage the late innings. The bullpen, once a supporting cast, became a central figure in the narrative of a baseball game.

Speed on the Basepaths: The Ground Ball Advantage

The introduction of artificial surfaces brought about a fundamental change in how players approached hitting. The faster and bouncier nature of these surfaces made it advantageous to hit ground balls in the gaps between corner and middle infielders. Teams recognized the potential for manufacturing runs through speed on the basepaths, shifting the offensive focus from power hitting to strategic baserunning.

As players adapted to the nuances of artificial turf, the stolen base became a potent offensive weapon. Teams strategically exploited the increased speed of the game, focusing on creating opportunities to advance runners through aggressive baserunning. The emphasis on speed ushered in an era where manufacturing runs through small ball became a strategic cornerstone.

The Demise of Complete Games: A New Era for Starting Pitchers

The expectation for starting pitchers to throw complete games waned during the 1980s. Instead, the emphasis shifted towards starters pitching 6–7 innings before handing over the game to the bullpen. This marked a departure from the era when starting pitchers were tasked with going the distance. The role of the closer gained prominence as teams sought specialists to secure victories in the final innings.

Starting pitchers were no longer burdened with the expectation of completing every game. The evolution in pitching strategy recognized the importance of preserving arms and strategically deploying pitchers based on situational advantages. The emergence of closers as pivotal figures showcased the changing dynamics of managing pitching staffs.

Stolen Bases vs. Home Runs: A Statistical Shift

As stolen bases surged, home run totals experienced a decline. After Willie Mays' remarkable 52-home run season in 1965, the following decades saw a scarcity of players reaching such milestones. The emphasis on speed and manufacturing runs through stolen bases contributed to a statistical shift that challenged the traditional dominance of power hitting.

The trade-off between stolen bases and home runs reflected a broader shift in offensive philosophy. Teams prioritized strategic baserunning over the long ball, recognizing the impact of speed on the basepaths. The statistical landscape of baseball underwent a transformation, reflecting the evolving priorities of teams and players.

Conclusion: Adapting to a New Baseball Reality

The 1980s marked a pivotal era of adaptation and innovation in baseball strategy. From the bullpen revolution to the strategic advantage of speed on artificial surfaces, teams navigated a changing landscape. As the dynamics of pitching and offense underwent a paradigm shift, baseball entered a new era where versatility and adaptability became crucial components of success. The legacy of this transformative period would resonate through subsequent decades, influencing how teams approached the intricacies of the game.

Chapter 33: Unraveling Scandals and the Shifting Game Dynamics

The 1980s unfolded as a decade of considerable change and upheaval in the landscape of baseball. From a decline in home run numbers to the emergence of scandalous incidents, this chapter unravels the intricate tapestry of baseball's evolution during this transformative period. As the game faced challenges both on and off the field, it grappled with issues that would leave a lasting impact on its narrative.

The Home Run Decline: A Departure from Power-Hitting Norms

The 1980s marked a departure from the power-hitting norms that had characterized previous eras of baseball. Unlike the prolific home run outputs of the 1960s and 1970s, the decade saw a decline in the number of players hitting 40 home runs or more. Strikingly, no player surpassed the iconic 50-home run mark in a single season, a trend not witnessed since the Dead-ball era (1900–1919).

The declining trend in home runs during the 1980s signaled a shift in offensive dynamics. Factors such as changes in player conditioning, alterations in pitching strategies, and a possible impact from the rise of artificial surfaces contributed to a recalibration of the power-hitting paradigm that had dominated the preceding decades.

The Cocaine Scandal: Dark Shadows Cast Over the Diamond

While the 1980s showcased on-field transformations, it was also marred by off-field controversies, most notably the cocaine scandal that cast dark shadows over the game. Several high-profile players faced allegations of drug abuse, raising questions about the integrity of the sport and the personal conduct of its athletes.

The cocaine scandal exposed vulnerabilities in baseball's cultural fabric. The revelations of drug abuse among players prompted a reckoning with the off-field challenges faced by the sport. Baseball authorities were compelled to address issues of substance abuse, leading to increased scrutiny, testing protocols, and educational programs aimed at safeguarding the integrity of the game.

Pete Rose and the Gambling Controversy: A Fall from Grace

Another seismic event that rocked baseball during the 1980s was the gambling controversy involving one of the game's most iconic figures, Pete Rose. The revelation that Rose, a celebrated player and manager, had engaged in gambling activities, including betting on his own team, sent shockwaves through the baseball community.

Pete Rose's fall from grace highlighted the fragility of baseball's moral compass. The gambling controversy prompted a reassessment of the relationship between players, managers, and the ethical standards expected in professional baseball. The repercussions of Rose's actions extended beyond his individual legacy, influencing discussions on the intersection of personal conduct and the sanctity of the game.

Conclusion: Navigating Turbulent Waters

The 1980s emerged as a decade of contrasts for baseball, marked by both on-field transformations and off-field controversies. As the game grappled with a decline in power-hitting traditions and confronted scandals that challenged its integrity, it also laid the groundwork for reforms and changes that would shape its future. The echoes of these events would reverberate through subsequent decades, underscoring the perpetual tension between the evolving nature of the sport and the enduring values that define it.

Chapter 34: A Game Interrupted - The 1981 MLB Strike

The year 1981 stands as a poignant chapter in the history of Major League Baseball, marked by a tumultuous period that would disrupt the regular rhythm of the game. The MLB strike, which unfolded from June 12 until July 31, left an indelible mark, forcing the cancellation of 713 total games and introducing an unprecedented split-season format.

The Prelude to the Strike: Labor Unrest and Dissatisfaction

As the 1981 season commenced, tensions between the Major League Baseball Players Association (MLBPA) and team owners reached a breaking point. A fundamental disagreement over compensation, particularly the issue of free agency, fueled a growing sense of discontent among players. The negotiations between the MLBPA and the owners failed to yield a resolution, setting the stage for what would become a protracted labor dispute.

The underlying tension stemmed from the players' desire for greater agency in determining their professional destinies. The concept of free agency, a contentious issue in the negotiations, symbolized the players' quest for autonomy and fair compensation.

The Strike Unfolds: A Halting of Baseball's Heartbeat

On June 12, 1981, the MLBPA, led by executive director Marvin Miller, called for a strike, bringing the regular season to an abrupt halt. The strike's immediate impact was felt across ballparks, with players walking away from the fields, leaving stadiums silent and fans bewildered.

The strike represented a stand-off between labor and management, with players collectively asserting their rights in the face of perceived injustices. The abrupt cessation of games left a void in the lives of fans who were accustomed to the rhythm of the baseball season, highlighting the sport's integral place in American culture.

Cancellation of Games: A Stark Reality for Players and Fans

As negotiations between the MLBPA and the owners lingered, the toll on the 1981 season became increasingly evident. A staggering total of 713 games were canceled during the strike, leaving players without the opportunity to compete and fans without the joy of witnessing their favorite teams in action.

The cancellation of games served as a stark reminder of the broader impact of labor disputes on the fabric of professional sports. Baseball, traditionally viewed as a source of entertainment and communal spirit, found itself at the center of a larger societal conversation about the rights of workers and the economic structures governing professional sports.

Introduction of the Split-Season Format: A Compromise Reached

Amid the impasse, a compromise known as the "split-season" format emerged. The season was divided into two halves, with the winners of each half in each division earning playoff berths. This innovative approach aimed to salvage some semblance of a competitive season while acknowledging the reality of the truncated schedule.

The split-season format, while unconventional, demonstrated the sport's resilience and its capacity for adaptation in the face of adversity. It introduced a unique competitive structure that added a layer of intrigue to the postseason race.

Aftermath and Legacy: Lessons Learned

The 1981 MLB strike eventually came to an end on July 31, with players and owners reaching a tentative agreement. While the strike had taken its toll on the season, it left a lasting legacy that would shape future labor relations in baseball.

The aftermath of the strike prompted reflections on the need for a more equitable and sustainable relationship between players and ownership. It underscored the delicate balance between the business of baseball and its status as a beloved pastime, with lessons learned that would echo through subsequent negotiations.

Conclusion: A Chapter in Flux

The 1981 MLB strike remains a chapter in baseball's narrative that evokes memories of labor strife, disrupted seasons, and the resilience of the sport in the face of challenges. As the game moved forward, it carried with it the lessons gleaned from this tumultuous period, shaping the ongoing dialogue about the intricate dance between players, owners, and the enduring spirit of America's pastime.

Chapter 35: Trials and Tribulations - Baseball's Complex 1980s Landscape

The 1980s in Major League Baseball were marked by both triumphs and controversies, encapsulating the essence of a sport grappling with its traditions while navigating the complexities of modern times. In 1985, Pete Rose etched his name in baseball history by breaking Ty Cobb's all-time hits record, a moment of celebration shadowed by the ominous clouds of the Pittsburgh drug trials. Furthermore, the year 1989 witnessed a seismic event as Rose, a baseball icon, received a lifetime ban for betting on games while managing the Cincinnati Reds.

Pete Rose's Historic Achievement: 4,192 and Counting

In the summer of 1985, the baseball world witnessed a milestone that had endured for over six decades. Pete Rose, a tenacious and prolific hitter, surpassed Ty Cobb's long-standing record of 4,191 hits, firmly establishing himself as the all-time hits leader with his 4,192nd hit.

Rose's achievement was a testament to his longevity, consistency, and unwavering commitment to the game. However, this triumph would soon be overshadowed by the revelation of his involvement in a scandal that would stain his legacy.

The Pittsburgh Drug Trials: Baseball Confronts Cocaine Scandal

Amid the on-field heroics and record-breaking moments, the Pittsburgh drug trials cast a dark shadow over the sport in 1985. Several players found themselves entangled in legal proceedings related to cocaine trafficking, as they were called to testify before a grand jury in Pittsburgh.

The drug trials exposed a seedy underbelly of the baseball world, revealing the challenges faced by players dealing with substance abuse. The trials prompted a reckoning within the league, forcing baseball to confront issues of addiction and the broader impact on the sport's reputation.

1989: Pete Rose's Banishment and the End of an Era

The year 1989 would forever alter the trajectory of Pete Rose's storied career. Rose, who had transitioned from player to manager, faced allegations of betting on baseball games, including those involving his own team, the Cincinnati Reds. The revelation led to a swift and unprecedented decision by then-Commissioner A. Bartlett Giamatti: Rose received a lifetime ban from baseball.

Rose's banishment was a seismic event, sending shockwaves through the baseball community. It raised questions about the integrity of the game, the responsibilities of those entrusted with its stewardship, and the consequences for those who violated its sacred trust.

Reflections on a Decade: Balancing Acts and Moral Dilemmas

As the 1980s drew to a close, Major League Baseball found itself at a crossroads. The decade had witnessed remarkable achievements on the field, but it was also marred by scandals that challenged the sport's moral fiber. The balance between celebration and scrutiny, triumphs and trials, underscored the complexities inherent in America's pastime.

The 1980s left an indelible mark on baseball's narrative, weaving together tales of triumph and tribulation. It prompted the sport to grapple with issues of morality, accountability, and the evolving landscape of professional athletics.

Conclusion: Navigating Turbulent Waters

The 1980s in baseball unfolded as a nuanced tale of highs and lows, records shattered and reputations tarnished. As the sport moved into a new decade, it carried the lessons learned from this era of trials and tribulations, laying the groundwork for a continuing dialogue about the essence of baseball and the delicate balance it maintains between tradition and transformation.

Chapter 36: A Lost Season - The Impact of the 1994–95 MLB Strike

The summer of 1994 was poised to be a defining moment in Major League Baseball, with the postseason on the horizon and teams vying for a shot at glory. However, the sport was plunged into darkness as the 1994–95 MLB strike unfolded, leading to the cancellation of over 900 games and the unprecedented forfeiture of the entire postseason.

The Precursors to Discontent: Labor Strife and Contract Disputes

In the years leading up to the strike, tensions simmered between Major League Baseball and the Major League Baseball Players Association (MLBPA). Disputes over revenue sharing, salary caps, and the overall economic structure of the league laid the groundwork for a labor dispute that would bring the sport to a grinding halt.

As the negotiations faltered, the impending strike loomed like a storm on the horizon, casting a shadow over the players, the teams, and the fans who had come to cherish the annual spectacle of postseason baseball.

August 12, 1994: The Day Baseball Stood Still

On August 12, 1994, the inevitable came to pass. Frustrated with the lack of progress in labor negotiations, the players initiated a strike that would echo through the caverns of ballparks and resonate across a nation of baseball enthusiasts. With this fateful decision, the season came to an abrupt halt, leaving stadiums eerily silent and fields deserted.

The strike was a profound moment in the history of baseball, marking the first time in 90 years that the postseason would be absent from the calendar. The very essence of the game, synonymous with resilience and continuity, was shattered.

The Fallout: Canceled Games, Forfeited Dreams

Over 900 games were erased from the schedule as the strike persisted, leaving baseball fans in a state of despair. The cherished traditions of pennant races, wild card chases, and the drama of October baseball were replaced by a void that seemed insurmountable. The strike became a symbol of a sport at odds with itself, caught in the crossfire of labor disputes.

As the calendar turned, the ghosts of a lost season haunted ballparks and the collective consciousness of fans, players, and stakeholders. The impact rippled beyond the diamond, affecting communities that thrived on the vitality of their home teams.

The Lingering Aftermath: A Game Transformed

The strike's resolution in April 1995 marked the end of a dark chapter, but the scars lingered. Baseball emerged from the shadows to a changed landscape. The absence of a postseason in 1994 left questions about what might have been, and the tarnished image of a sport in conflict needed mending.

The strike left an indelible mark on the psyche of baseball, prompting reflection on the balance between commerce and competition. The wounds would heal, but the legacy of the lost season would forever shape the narrative of Major League Baseball.

Conclusion: A Lesson Learned, a Price Paid

The 1994–95 MLB strike stands as a cautionary tale in the annals of baseball history. It serves as a reminder of the delicate equilibrium that must be maintained between the players, the league, and the fans. The cost of a lost season went beyond financial implications, delving into the very soul of the sport.

As baseball moved forward, the scars of the strike became part of its narrative, influencing future negotiations and shaping the way the game approached labor relations. The lost season was a harsh lesson, but one that would, in time, contribute to a renewed appreciation for the resilience of America's pastime.

Chapter 37: A Controversial Epoch - The Steroid Era, Further Expansion, and Near Contraction

In the late 1990s and early 2000s, Major League Baseball experienced a seismic shift in offensive production. The era witnessed an unprecedented number of players consistently hitting 40 or 50 home runs in a single season, challenging the notions of what was considered attainable in the realm of power-hitting. However, beneath the awe-inspiring feats on the field lurked a controversial secret that would cast a long shadow over the sport.

The Power Surge: Records Shattered and Fans Awestruck

During the late 1990s, names like Mark McGwire and Sammy Sosa became synonymous with home run heroics. The 1998 season, in particular, captured the imagination of fans as McGwire and Sosa engaged in a historic home run chase, both surpassing Roger Maris's long-standing record of 61 home runs in a single season. McGwire finished with 70, while Sosa closely trailed with 66, forever etching their names in the annals of baseball history.

The electrifying displays of power thrilled fans and revitalized interest in the game. Baseball was enjoying a renaissance, with attendance soaring and television ratings reaching new heights.

The Revelation: The Dark Side of Glory

As the echoes of cheering fans reverberated through ballparks, a cloud of suspicion hung over the sport. In the aftermath of the power surge, revelations about the use of performance-enhancing drugs, particularly steroids, began to emerge. Players previously celebrated for their extraordinary achievements faced accusations and investigations, tarnishing the integrity of the game.

The steroid era cast a pall over the accomplishments of those years, calling into question the legitimacy of records and achievements. The awe once reserved for towering home runs now mingled with skepticism and disappointment.

The Mitchell Report: Unveiling a Troubled Era

In 2007, former Senator George J. Mitchell released a comprehensive report, known as the Mitchell Report, documenting the pervasive use of performance-enhancing drugs in baseball. The report implicated numerous players, exposing the extent of the issue and prompting a reckoning within the baseball community.

The Mitchell Report was a watershed moment, forcing baseball to confront the challenges posed by performance-enhancing substances and prompting a collective effort to clean up the sport.

Expansion and Near Contraction: A Dueling Narrative

While the steroid era unfolded, Major League Baseball was also navigating the complexities of expansion and the specter of contraction. The addition of teams like the Arizona Diamondbacks and Tampa Bay Devil Rays expanded the league's footprint, bringing baseball to new markets. However, financial challenges and discussions about potentially contracting struggling franchises added a layer of uncertainty to the league's landscape.

The dual narrative of expansion and near contraction reflected the evolving nature of Major League Baseball, a sport grappling with both its successes and the shadows cast by controversies.

Conclusion: Lessons Learned, Legacy Defined

The steroid era stands as a paradox in baseball's history—a period of remarkable achievements overshadowed by the taint of performance-enhancing drugs. The era forced baseball to confront its vulnerabilities, leading to significant changes in drug testing protocols and a renewed commitment to the integrity of the game.

As baseball moved into the 21st century, the lessons learned from the steroid era became integral to shaping a new narrative—one that prioritized transparency, accountability, and the preservation of the sport's essence.

Chapter 38: Expanding Horizons - The Birth of the Marlins, Rockies, Diamondbacks, and Devil Rays

The 1990s marked a period of expansion and realignment for Major League Baseball, as the league sought to broaden its horizons, reaching new markets and welcoming fresh franchises into the fold. This chapter delves into the transformative events of 1993 and 1998 when the Florida Marlins, Colorado Rockies, Arizona Diamondbacks, and Tampa Bay Devil Rays made their debut, adding a new chapter to the ever-evolving story of America's pastime.

1993: Marlins Dive into the League

In 1993, the National League set the stage for a major expansion, welcoming the Florida Marlins into the league. Based in Miami, the Marlins represented the first MLB team in the Sunshine State. The arrival of the Marlins brought baseball to a region known for its vibrant culture and diverse demographics. The team's teal and orange colors quickly became synonymous with the tropical allure of Florida.

The Marlins' inaugural season was a pivotal moment for baseball, establishing a presence in a dynamic and rapidly growing market. The move was not only a geographical expansion but also a cultural one, reflecting baseball's commitment to embracing diverse communities.

1993: Rockies Reach New Heights in Denver

Simultaneously, the National League witnessed the addition of the Colorado Rockies, making Denver the home of a Major League Baseball team for the first time. Nestled against the backdrop of the Rocky Mountains, the Rockies brought baseball to the high-altitude terrain of Colorado. The team's purple and silver color scheme mirrored the majestic landscapes that surrounded their home ballpark.

The Rockies' entry into the league extended baseball's footprint into the mountainous landscapes of the West, captivating fans with the allure of baseball played against the breathtaking backdrop of the Rockies.

1998: Brewers Change Leagues, Diamondbacks Rise in Phoenix, Devil Rays Illuminate Tampa Bay

As the late 1990s unfolded, further changes reshaped the league's landscape. The Milwaukee Brewers made a historic move by switching leagues, leaving the American League to join the National League. This move marked a departure from convention, adding a new layer of intrigue to league dynamics.

Meanwhile, 1998 witnessed the birth of two new franchises—one in the arid landscapes of Phoenix and the other in the sun-soaked region of Tampa Bay. The Arizona Diamondbacks and Tampa Bay Devil Rays brought baseball to the desert and the Gulf Coast, respectively.

Legacy of Expansion: A Rich Tapestry Unfurls

The expansion of the 1990s left an indelible mark on Major League Baseball. New teams brought fresh energy, expanded the league's geographic reach, and forged connections with communities eager to embrace the national pastime. The Marlins, Rockies, Diamondbacks, and Devil Rays were not just additions to the league; they were catalysts for a new era of growth and diversity.

The legacy of expansion extends beyond the box scores, weaving a rich tapestry that reflects the ever-evolving nature of baseball—a sport that continually seeks to captivate the hearts of fans across the nation.

Chapter 39: Averted Crisis - Contraction Controversy and the Survival of the Expos and Twins

At the conclusion of the 2001 MLB season, the specter of contraction loomed over Major League Baseball, threatening the existence of long-standing franchises. This chapter explores the controversial proposal to contract teams, with a particular focus on the Montreal Expos and the Minnesota Twins, two teams that faced the imminent threat of dissolution.

The Contraction Proposal: A Radical Shift in MLB's Landscape

In the wake of the 2001 season, team owners collectively voted in favor of contraction, a drastic measure aimed at reducing the number of teams in Major League Baseball. While several teams were initially considered for elimination, the Montreal Expos and the Minnesota Twins emerged as the primary targets in the proposed contraction plan.

The contraction proposal sent shockwaves through the baseball community, sparking debates about the economic viability of certain franchises and the potential impact on the league's competitive balance.

Expos on the Brink: Montreal's Baseball Future in Peril

For the Montreal Expos, contraction posed an existential threat. The team, already grappling with attendance challenges and financial difficulties, faced the prospect of being erased from the league. The vibrant baseball culture in Montreal, a city with a rich history in the sport, teetered on the edge of extinction.

Montreal, once a proud home to baseball legends and passionate fans, confronted the harsh reality that the Expos might cease to exist, leaving a void in the hearts of devoted supporters.

Twins Fight for Survival: A Legal Battle Ensues

In Minnesota, the Twins confronted their own battle for survival. Plans for contraction were temporarily halted when the team's landlord secured a court injunction, mandating that the Twins play their 2002 home games at the Metrodome. This legal maneuver injected a temporary reprieve, allowing the Twins to continue their legacy on the field.

As the legal drama unfolded, the Twins fought not only to preserve their franchise but also to maintain the strong baseball tradition in Minnesota, where the team held a special place in the hearts of fans.

League-Wide Backlash and Reprieve

Amidst growing opposition from players, fans, and baseball stakeholders, MLB owners ultimately agreed to postpone any reduction in the league's size until at least 2006. The contraction plan, initially poised to reshape the landscape of professional baseball, faced a wave of backlash that forced a reconsideration of its implications.

The near-contraction of the Expos and Twins underscored the delicate balance between financial considerations and the preservation of baseball's cultural and historical significance.

Conclusion: A Lesson Learned and the Future Unfolds

The chapter concludes with reflections on the contraction controversy, highlighting the tension between economic considerations and the intangible value of baseball franchises within the fabric of American culture. The survival of the Expos and Twins serves as a testament to the enduring resilience of teams facing adversity and the unwavering passion of baseball communities. As the league grappled with its future, lessons learned from this contentious period would shape decisions and discussions in the years to come.

Chapter 40: Franchise Exodus - The Montreal Expos Relocate to Washington

In 2005, the Montreal Expos made history by becoming the first Major League Baseball franchise to relocate in over three decades. This significant move not only reshaped the baseball landscape but also stirred debates about the factors leading to the departure of a team with a storied past. This chapter delves into the circumstances surrounding the relocation of the Expos, their transformation into the Washington Nationals, and the implications for both cities involved.

The Montreal Expos Legacy: A Tale of Unfulfilled Potential

Montreal, a city rich in cultural diversity and passion for sports, had been the proud home of the Expos since their inception in 1969. However, despite moments of brilliance and a dedicated fan base, the Expos struggled with attendance issues, financial challenges, and an uncertain future in their later years. The team's legacy was marked by unfulfilled potential, leaving fans to ponder what might have been.

The Expos' departure from Montreal symbolized the end of an era, leaving a void in the hearts of fans who had supported the team through its highs and lows.

Baseball's Return to Washington: Nationals Take the Stage

The relocation of the Expos meant the return of Major League Baseball to Washington, D.C. after a 33-year absence. The nation's capital, once home to the Washington Senators, welcomed the new incarnation of the franchise—the Washington Nationals. The move sparked excitement and anticipation among baseball enthusiasts in Washington, eager to embrace their new team and create fresh memories.

For Washingtonians, the arrival of the Nationals represented not just the acquisition of a baseball team but a reconnection with a sport that held a special place in the city's history.

City Reclaimed: Baseball's Return to Abandoned Territories

Baseball has a unique tendency to return to cities that were once abandoned. The relocation of franchises, a recurrent theme in MLB history, often involves the revival of baseball in places that had experienced loss and departure. The return of the Nationals to Washington echoed this pattern, rekindling the spirit of a city that had longed for the sights and sounds of baseball.

The cyclical nature of baseball's presence in cities mirrored the ebb and flow of the sport's popularity and the ever-changing dynamics of the league.

Montreal's Lonely Status: A City Without a Team

In the aftermath of the Expos' relocation, Montreal found itself in a peculiar position. As of December 2022, the city remains the only one, not counting the short-lived Federal League, to have hosted an MLB franchise since 1901 without currently having a team. The void left by the Expos' departure lingered, prompting discussions about the feasibility of bringing baseball back to Montreal.

Montreal's status as a city without an MLB team raised questions about the challenges and opportunities in reestablishing a baseball presence in a city with a deep-rooted connection to the sport.

Conclusion: A Chapter Closes, Another Begins

The relocation of the Montreal Expos to Washington marked a significant chapter in the ongoing narrative of Major League Baseball. The departure of a team with a unique history and the emergence of the Nationals in a new setting reflected the dynamic nature of the sport. As baseball continued to evolve, the legacy of the Expos persisted in the memories of Montreal fans, while Washington embraced a new era of baseball with hope and anticipation for the future.

Chapter 41: The Modern Game - A Technological Revolution

In recent years, Major League Baseball (MLB) has undergone a transformative evolution, propelled by cutting-edge technologies that have reshaped the way the game is played, analyzed, and experienced. This chapter delves into the modern era of baseball, exploring the impact of technologies like Statcast and Hawk-Eye on player performance, strategic decision-making, and the fan experience.

Statcast Unveiled: Revolutionizing Player Analysis

The introduction of Statcast has emerged as a game-changer in the world of baseball. Deployed in recent years, Statcast employs a sophisticated radar and camera system to capture precise data on player movements, offering unprecedented insights into the mechanics of pitching, hitting, and fielding. Teams now have access to a wealth of information that goes beyond traditional statistics, enabling a deeper understanding of player performance.

Statcast's revolutionary capabilities have opened new frontiers in player analysis, empowering teams to refine strategies and unlock the full potential of their athletes.

The Hawk-Eye Phenomenon: A New Dimension to Umpiring

Since 2020, the integration of Hawk-Eye technology has added a layer of precision to umpiring decisions. This system employs cameras to track the trajectory of the ball, providing an accurate and instant assessment of whether a pitch is a ball or strike. The implementation of Hawk-Eye aims to enhance the accuracy of officiating, reducing the margin for human error and contributing to fairer outcomes on the field.

Hawk-Eye's role in umpiring has not only improved the accuracy of calls but has also sparked discussions about the balance between technology and the human element in the game.

Advanced Statistics: Unveiling the Nuances of Performance

In parallel with technological advancements, platforms like FanGraphs and Baseball Savant have become integral to the modern baseball landscape. These websites offer a plethora of advanced statistics, ranging from exit velocity and launch angle to defensive metrics and pitch tracking. Fans, analysts, and teams alike now have access to a comprehensive suite of metrics that provide a nuanced understanding of player contributions beyond traditional stats.

The era of advanced statistics has democratized baseball insights, allowing enthusiasts to engage with the game on a deeper level and challenging conventional notions of player value.

Defensive Analytics: Decoding the Art of Fielding

One of the remarkable outcomes of Statcast's capabilities is the emergence of advanced defensive analytics. Fielding, traditionally subjective and challenging to quantify, is now subjected to objective scrutiny. Statcast's ability to track player movements allows for a more accurate assessment of defensive prowess, enabling teams to optimize their defensive alignments and strategies.

Defensive analytics represent a paradigm shift, turning a once subjective aspect of the game into a quantifiable and strategic asset for teams.

The Fan Experience: A New Dimension of Engagement

Beyond its impact on teams and players, the technological revolution has significantly enhanced the fan experience. Real-time data, visualizations, and interactive tools have become integral components of how fans consume and engage with the game. Whether attending a ballpark or watching from home, enthusiasts now have access to a wealth of information that enriches their understanding and enjoyment of baseball.

The modern fan is immersed in a dynamic and data-rich baseball experience, fostering a deeper connection to the sport and its evolving narratives.

Conclusion: A Technological Odyssey Unfolds

As Major League Baseball strides into the modern era, the fusion of technology and the national pastime continues to redefine the contours of the game. From advanced player analysis to precise officiating and an enriched fan experience, the impact of technologies like Statcast and Hawk-Eye is indelibly shaping the narrative of baseball. As the sport navigates this technological odyssey, the possibilities for innovation and discovery appear boundless, promising an exciting and dynamic future for America's favorite pastime.

Chapter 42: Shifting Sands - Defensive Strategies and MLB's Evolution

In recent years, Major League Baseball (MLB) has witnessed a seismic shift in defensive strategies, with teams increasingly deploying the defensive shift to counter hitters' tendencies. This chapter explores the evolution of the defensive shift, the impact of advanced statistics on its prevalence, and MLB's response to this tactical transformation.

The Rise of the Defensive Shift: A Statistical Approach

The deployment of the defensive shift has become a defining trend in contemporary baseball, driven by a surge in the use of advanced statistics. Teams, armed with a wealth of data on hitters' tendencies, have strategically positioned fielders to counteract the expected trajectory of batted balls. The shift aims to exploit statistical probabilities, reducing the likelihood of hits and altering the dynamics of the game.

The defensive shift's ascent, from a tactic employed in specific situations to a pervasive strategy, reflects baseball's growing reliance on data-driven decision-making.

Statistical Surge: From 2016 to 2022

A key catalyst for the defensive shift's prevalence has been the surge in its usage, as evidenced by statistical trends from 2016 to 2022. The adoption rate skyrocketed from 13.7% in 2016 to a staggering 33.6% in 2022. This surge underscores teams' increasing confidence in the shift as an effective tool for neutralizing opposing hitters. The embrace of advanced metrics has empowered teams to make strategic decisions that transcend traditional defensive alignments.

The exponential rise in shift usage signifies a paradigm shift in how teams approach defense, leveraging statistical insights to gain a competitive edge.

MLB's Response: Banning Extreme Infield Shifts

As the defensive shift became ubiquitous, MLB found itself at a crossroads, balancing the pursuit of strategic innovation with the desire to enhance the entertainment value of the game. In a groundbreaking move, MLB announced in September 2022 that extreme infield defensive shifts would be banned starting in 2023. This decision reflected a nuanced approach to maintaining a delicate equilibrium between strategic sophistication and fan engagement.

MLB's ban on extreme shifts signals a commitment to preserving the balance between offense and defense, aiming to sustain fan interest in the face of evolving tactics.

Regulatory Framework: Two Fielders on Each Side of Second Base

The regulatory framework for the defensive shift ban is clear and concise. To be compliant, teams must position two fielders on each side of second base, with both players having both feet on the infield dirt at the time the pitch is thrown. Failure to adhere to this rule presents consequences for the defensive team, with the batting team granted the choice of an automatic ball or the outcome of the play.

MLB's regulatory guidelines emphasize the importance of maintaining defensive integrity while injecting a degree of predictability into the game.

Impact on the Game: Balancing Strategy and Spectacle

As MLB implements the ban on extreme infield shifts, the baseball community awaits the repercussions on the dynamics of the game. While the shift has been a strategic masterstroke, its proliferation raised concerns about diminishing offensive excitement. The ban represents a delicate compromise, aiming to foster a balance where strategic ingenuity coexists with the thrill of hits and runs.

The ban's impact on the game's rhythm and narrative underscores the ongoing quest for equilibrium between tactical sophistication and fan-centric entertainment.

Conclusion: Navigating the Future of Defensive Tactics

The defensive shift's journey from a sporadic ploy to a ubiquitous strategy encapsulates baseball's perpetual quest for innovation. As MLB navigates the terrain of defensive tactics, the ban on extreme shifts stands as a testament to the league's commitment to preserving the essence of the sport. How this decision shapes the future of defensive strategies and the fan experience remains an unfolding narrative, emblematic of baseball's enduring capacity for evolution.

Chapter 43: Pacing the Diamond - MLB's Battle Against Game Slowness

Baseball, once celebrated for its leisurely pace and strategic nuances, is grappling with a contemporary challenge—sluggish game speed. This chapter delves into the factors contributing to the deceleration of baseball games, the implications of extended durations, and Major League Baseball's (MLB) proactive measures, including the introduction of a pitch clock for the 2023 season.

The Creeping Slowdown: A Time Analysis

The leisurely pace of baseball has come under scrutiny as game durations have steadily increased. In 2020, the average time to complete a nine-inning game stretched to three hours and six minutes, marking a continuous upward trend over the years. The proliferation of strikeouts, walks, and the prolonged time taken by pitchers to deliver each pitch has contributed to the game's deceleration.

As the sands of time accumulate on the diamond, concerns over the potential impact on fan engagement and the overall viewing experience have prompted MLB to address the issue head-on.

Defensive Shifts and the Tactical Chess Game

The rise of defensive shifts, a strategic chess move aimed at neutralizing hitters, has been a contributing factor to the elongation of games. While shifts showcase the analytical depth of the sport, they often lead to prolonged at-bats, with hitters adjusting their approach to counter the strategic realignment of fielders. As MLB navigates the delicate balance between strategy and spectacle, it recognizes the need to curtail the excesses that may compromise the game's inherent allure.

The strategic dance between batters and fielders, while adding a layer of complexity to the game, has inadvertently become a contributor to extended game durations.

The Dawn of the Pitch Clock Era

In response to the escalating concerns about game length, MLB has chosen to implement a pitch clock for the 2023 season. Borrowing from the successful experiment in Minor League Baseball (MiLB), the pitch clock introduces a time constraint at various stages of the pitcher-batter interaction. Starting at 15 seconds, the clock triggers a sequence of events designed to expedite the game without compromising its essence.

The pitch clock serves as a time guardian, ushering in a new era where strategic brilliance must coexist with a heightened sense of urgency.

Navigating the Pitch Clock: Rules and Penalties

The mechanics of the pitch clock are intricate, outlining specific deadlines for players involved in the pitcher-batter exchange. If the catcher is not in their crouch behind home plate by the time the clock reaches 10 seconds, the defending team faces an additional ball. Simultaneously, a batter's failure to be "alert" in the batter's box by the 8-second mark results in an extra strike. To prevent abuse, pickoffs and step-offs that reset the pitch clock are limited, adding layers of strategy and consequence.

The introduction of the pitch clock introduces a dynamic element to the game, prompting players and teams to adapt to a more time-conscious playing environment.

Balancing Act: Timeout Restrictions and the Future Landscape

To ensure that the pitch clock achieves its intended purpose, MLB has imposed restrictions on timeouts. A batter is granted only one timeout per plate appearance, serving as a reset button for the pitch clock. This limitation aims to curb intentional disruptions and maintain a flow that aligns with the pace-of-play objectives.

The confluence of pitch clock regulations and timeout restrictions paints a picture of a game seeking equilibrium between strategy, tradition, and contemporary expectations.

Conclusion: A Time-Tested Game Adapts

As MLB embraces the pitch clock era, baseball stands at a crossroads, navigating the delicate balance between tradition and the evolving expectations of a modern audience. The quest to rejuvenate the pace of play underscores the dynamic nature of a sport deeply rooted in history yet unafraid to adapt. Whether the pitch clock becomes a timeless addition or a fleeting experiment, it reflects the enduring spirit of baseball—a game that bends without breaking, forever bound by the passage of time on the diamond.

Chapter 44: Unraveling the Sign-Stealing Scandal

The purity of baseball's competitive spirit faced a severe test in 2019 when MLB launched an investigation into allegations of sign-stealing by the Houston Astros, culminating in a revelation that sent shockwaves through the baseball community. This chapter delves into the intricate details of the sign-stealing scandal that tarnished the reputation of the 2017 World Series champion Astros and implicated another prominent team, the Boston Red Sox.

The Allegations Unveiled: A Quest for Unfair Advantage

In the heart of the scandal were allegations that members of the Houston Astros illicitly stole signs from opposing teams using technology during the 2017 and 2018 seasons. Sign-stealing, a practice as old as the game itself, took an insidious turn as advanced technologies became tools to gain an unfair advantage. The investigation, prompted by concerns raised by players, fans, and the broader baseball community, sought to unearth the truth behind the allegations.

As the revelations unfolded, the integrity of the game hung in the balance, with the sign-stealing scandal exposing a darker side of competition in the MLB.

Guilty Verdict: Astros and the Fallout

In January 2020, the verdict was delivered—the Houston Astros were found guilty of engaging in a systematic sign-stealing scheme. While no active players faced repercussions due to an immunity agreement in exchange for testimony, the impact reverberated through the leadership ranks. Astros general manager Jeff Luhnow and field manager A. J. Hinch faced substantial consequences, with both being suspended for the entire 2020 season.

The guilty verdict sent shockwaves through the baseball world, prompting reflections on the evolving relationship between technology and the age-old art of sign-stealing.

The Price of Deception: Penalties for the Astros

The penalties imposed on the Astros underscored the severity of their transgressions. The team was fined the maximum allowable amount of $5 million—a symbolic rebuke reflecting the gravity of the violations. Additionally, the Astros were forced to forfeit their first- and second-round picks in the 2020 and 2021 drafts, significantly impacting their ability to replenish talent through the draft.

The financial and strategic penalties served as a stark reminder that actions aimed at compromising the integrity of the game would not go unpunished.

A Broader Canvas: Red Sox Entangled

The sign-stealing investigation cast a wider net, ensnaring another successful franchise—the Boston Red Sox. Similar allegations of sign-stealing during the 2017 and 2018 seasons came to light, with the Red Sox's triumph in the 2018 World Series now tainted. The fallout for the Red Sox was swift, as manager Alex Cora, a central figure in the scandal, was handed a one-year suspension. The team also faced financial consequences, being fined and losing a second-round draft pick in the 2020 draft.

The Red Sox's entanglement in the scandal added another layer of complexity, emphasizing the need for vigilance in upholding the sport's integrity.

Conclusion: Rebuilding Trust and Preserving the Game

The sign-stealing scandal of 2019 and its aftermath served as a crucible, testing MLB's commitment to preserving the integrity of the game. As the implicated teams grappled with the fallout and the league implemented measures to prevent future transgressions, the episode underscored the constant tension between competition and sportsmanship. Baseball, resilient in the face of challenges, faced the task of rebuilding trust among fans and reiterating its commitment to a fair and untarnished playing field.

Chapter 45: The Athletics' Exodus: From Oakland to the Neon Lights of Las Vegas

In a surprising turn of events that reverberated through the baseball world, the Oakland Athletics, a storied franchise with a history intertwined with the city of Oakland, announced a seismic shift—relocating to the vibrant and iconic city of Las Vegas, Nevada. This chapter explores the factors, implications, and emotions surrounding the Athletics' decision to uproot and embark on a new chapter in the glittering desert oasis.

Farewell to the Bay Area: Oakland's Baseball Legacy

The Athletics' decision to leave the Bay Area marked the end of a rich baseball legacy that spanned decades. From the "Mustache Gang" era to the powerhouse teams of the late '80s, Oakland became synonymous with the green and gold. The team's connection with the city went beyond the diamond, intertwining with the community and forging a bond that seemed unbreakable.

The departure of the Athletics from Oakland left a void, not just in the MLB landscape, but in the hearts of loyal fans who had supported the team through thick and thin.

Las Vegas Beckons: A New Frontier for the Athletics

Las Vegas, a city renowned for its dazzling lights, entertainment, and a burgeoning sports scene, emerged as the surprising destination for the Athletics. The move signified a bold step into uncharted territory, as the franchise sought to establish itself in a city known more for hosting heavyweight title fights and superstar residencies than for its baseball traditions.

The allure of Las Vegas posed both opportunities and challenges, raising questions about how a city famous for spectacle would embrace America's pastime.

Factors Behind the Move: The Business of Baseball

Baseball, in its modern incarnation, operates at the intersection of sport and business. The Athletics' decision to relocate stemmed from a complex interplay of financial considerations, stadium woes, and the ever-evolving dynamics of professional sports. The quest for state-of-the-art facilities and increased revenue streams often clashes with the sentimental attachment fans have to a team's roots.

The move to Las Vegas reflected the pragmatic realities of contemporary baseball, where the quest for sustainability sometimes necessitates difficult choices.

Community Backlash: A Fractured Fanbase

The news of the Athletics' impending move triggered a wave of emotions among fans, with the loyal Oakland faithful expressing a mix of disappointment, anger, and a sense of abandonment. Franchise relocation is not merely a shift in geography but a rupture in the emotional connection between a team and its community.

The fractured fanbase raised broader questions about the balance between the business imperatives of sports franchises and their responsibilities to the communities that support them.

MLB's Shifting Landscape: Implications for the League

The Athletics' relocation adds another layer to the ongoing narrative of franchises seeking new homes in pursuit of growth and sustainability. As MLB grapples with the evolving dynamics of franchise locations, questions arise about the league's responsibility in ensuring the stability of teams in their existing markets and the impact of these moves on the broader baseball landscape.

The move of the Athletics reflects a larger trend in professional sports, prompting discussions about the delicate equilibrium between tradition and the pursuit of new horizons.

Conclusion: A New Chapter Unfolds

The relocation of the Oakland Athletics to Las Vegas marks a significant juncture in the team's history and the broader narrative of baseball's evolution. As the neon lights of Las Vegas beckon, the Athletics face the challenge of not only establishing themselves in a new city but also navigating the delicate task of winning over a fanbase that still mourns the loss of a team that was, for many years, an integral part of the fabric of Oakland. The story of the Athletics' move to Las Vegas is a chapter in the ever-evolving saga of baseball, where the pursuit of success and sustainability intersects with the deeply rooted emotions of fans and the storied histories of the cities they leave behind.

Chapter 46: The Evolution of Baseball Uniforms

The baseball uniform stands as a beacon, a visual embodiment of the sport's essence. Its metamorphosis from functional garb to a symbol of team identity mirrors the intricate journey of baseball itself. In this chapter, we embark on a comprehensive exploration of the evolution, innovation, and controversies surrounding baseball uniforms, each stitch narrating a chapter in the sport's rich history.

The Pioneering Days: Knickerbockers and the Birth of Tradition

The inception of baseball uniforms dates back to April 4, 1849, when the New York Knickerbockers took to the field in blue wool pants, white flannel shirts, and straw hats. This historic moment not only marked the birth of baseball attire but also set the stage for the uniform's symbolic role in the game. Caps and headgear were early companions, reflecting a time when there were no strict regulations on headwear.

The Knickerbockers, in their humble yet revolutionary outfits, laid the foundation for what would become an iconic part of baseball culture. The simplicity of their blue and white ensemble became a canvas on which teams would later paint their unique identities. As the sport gained popularity, the need for a standardized uniform emerged, leading to a visual transformation that would echo through the annals of baseball history.

Aesthetic Flourish: Stripes, Colors, and Team Identity Unveiled

The late 1880s witnessed a visual revolution as teams like Detroit, Washington, and Brooklyn introduced bold stripes to their uniforms. This departure from a mishmash of colors based on positions signaled a shift towards team-specific visual identities. Stripes became more than just a design element; they were a proclamation of team allegiance, contributing to the aesthetic appeal of the sport.

The introduction of stripes was more than a fashion statement; it was a strategic move to enhance team identity on the field. Players clad in distinctive striped uniforms became easily recognizable, and fans could passionately rally behind their team colors. The evolution of uniform aesthetics mirrored the growth of baseball into a professional and organized sport.

Dual Identities: Home and Away Uniforms

By the end of the 19th century, baseball adopted a dualistic approach to uniforms, with teams donning distinct attire for home and away games. The visual language of white pants and vests for home games and gray attire for away games became a standard across major leagues. This dual identity not only facilitated team identification but also added a layer of tradition to the evolving aesthetics of baseball.

The establishment of home and away uniforms was a practical response to the challenges posed by traveling between different ballparks. It served a functional purpose while contributing to the unique visual spectacle of baseball. The crisp whites worn on home turf and the subdued grays worn on the road became an integral part of the game's lore, embodying the spirit of competition and camaraderie.

Throwbacks and Modern Dynamics: Nostalgia Meets Contemporary Challenges

In recent decades, baseball uniforms have embraced a nostalgic revival, with teams incorporating throwback designs to honor the sport's heritage. Alternate uniforms featuring primary or secondary team colors have become a bridge connecting fans and players across different eras. Yet, the modern era introduces new dynamics, exemplified by cryptocurrency sponsorships like the FTX deal in 2021. The marriage of sports and finance, while innovative, also underscores the potential pitfalls as seen in FTX's bankruptcy in 2022.

The resurgence of throwback uniforms is a testament to baseball's enduring connection with its past. Teams don these retro designs as a nod to the legends who graced the diamond in eras gone by. The revival of classic aesthetics serves as a powerful link between generations of fans, fostering a sense of continuity and shared history.

Innovation and Controversies: Technology's Impact on Tradition

The intersection of technology and tradition is palpable in the realm of baseball uniforms. Smart fabrics, moisture-wicking materials, and advanced manufacturing techniques have redefined player comfort and performance. However, this influx of technology has not been without controversies. The delicate balance between honoring tradition and embracing cutting-edge advancements sparks debates within the baseball community.

As technology infiltrates every aspect of our lives, baseball is no exception. Uniforms, once crafted from wool and flannel, now incorporate cutting-edge materials designed to enhance players' physical performance. Moisture-wicking fabrics keep players cool under pressure, and ergonomic designs ensure optimal mobility. While these advancements are celebrated for their practical benefits, they also pose challenges to the cherished traditions of the sport.

Conclusion: Unraveling Threads of Legacy and Future Possibilities

In conclusion, the baseball uniform remains a tapestry of history, innovation, and identity. From the pioneering days of the Knickerbockers to the nuanced dynamics of modern sponsorships, each uniform tells a story. As the sport continues to evolve, so will its iconic attire, weaving together threads of legacy and future possibilities, forever stitched into the fabric of baseball's narrative.

Conclusion: A Tapestry of Triumphs, Challenges, and Enduring Legacy

In this comprehensive journey through the history of Major League Baseball, we have traversed the diamond, exploring the multifaceted story that unfolds inning after inning, season after season. The annals of baseball history are not merely a chronicle of wins and losses; they are a testament to the resilience, evolution, and enduring spirit of America's pastime.

The Birth Pangs: From Sandlots to Stadiums

Our odyssey begins in the sandlots of mid-19th century America, where baseball germinated as an informal pastime. From these humble origins, a phenomenon was born. The Knickerbockers took the inaugural step onto the field, clad in wool and straw hats, laying the foundation for the iconic baseball uniform. The evolution of uniforms became a visual journey, reflecting not just changes in fashion but also the sport's professionalization.

A League of Their Own: The Formation and Expansion of Major League Baseball

The birth of Major League Baseball marked the institutionalization of the sport, and the National League emerged as the vanguard. We witnessed the growth of the league, from its eight-team inception to the dynamic expansion that saw new franchises sprout across the nation. The migration to the West Coast heralded a new era, transforming baseball into a truly nationwide phenomenon.

The Roaring Twenties: Baseball's Golden Age

The Roaring Twenties catapulted baseball into its Golden Age, where legends like Babe Ruth and Lou Gehrig became synonymous with greatness. The saga of the 1927 Yankees, hailed as one of the greatest teams in history, unfolded against the backdrop of societal upheavals. This era solidified baseball's position as the nation's pastime, an emblem of hope and joy during challenging times.

The Dark Days: Baseball Through the Great Depression and World War II

Amidst economic turmoil and the global upheaval of World War II, baseball stood as a resilient pillar. The exodus of players to military service reshaped the landscape of the game, making room for unconventional heroes like Pete Gray, the one-armed outfielder. The war's impact extended to the diamond's illumination, as blackout restrictions threatened the very existence of night games.

Branch Rickey's Noble Experiment: Breaking the Color Barrier

Branch Rickey's audacious move to integrate baseball marked a watershed moment. Jackie Robinson's entry into the major leagues shattered racial barriers, sparking a seismic shift in the sport's landscape. The courageous journey of Robinson, facing prejudice and adversity, opened the door for countless African-American players and forever altered the trajectory of baseball's narrative.

The Expansion Era: Shifting Landscapes and New Frontiers

Baseball's relentless march forward brought about expansion, relocation, and a transformation of its geographic footprint. The move to the West Coast and the addition of new teams expanded the league's horizons. Simultaneously, the strike threat and subsequent suspension showcased the delicate balance between players and management in this evolving landscape.

Pitching Dominance and Rule Changes: Shaping the Game in the Late 1960s

The late 1960s witnessed a seismic shift in the balance between pitching and hitting, prompting rule changes to restore equilibrium. The reduction of the strike zone and the lowering of the pitcher's mound aimed to counter the dominance of pitchers.

This era laid the groundwork for further adjustments to maintain the delicate equilibrium between offense and defense.

Integration Spreads: African-American Players in the Major Leagues

Larry Doby's breakthrough in the American League and the addition of other black players signaled a broader wave of integration. Satchel Paige, Roy Campanella, and Don Newcombe joined the ranks, contributing their extraordinary talents to the game. The inclusion of these players not only diversified the talent pool but also added new dimensions to baseball's narrative.

Scandals and a Changing Game: Reflections on the 1980s

The 1980s brought about significant changes, from Pete Rose's record-breaking hits to the Pittsburgh drug trials. The era, marked by declining home run numbers, laid the groundwork for the scandals that would later rock the baseball world. The emergence of drug-related controversies highlighted the evolving dynamics within the sport.

The 1994–95 Strike: A Dark Chapter in Baseball History

The 1994–95 strike cast a shadow over the game, leading to the cancellation of games and the forfeiture of the entire postseason. The labor dispute showcased the complexities of the relationship between players and owners, leaving a lasting impact on both the league and its fans.

Steroid Era, Expansion, and Contraction: The Turn of the Millennium

The turn of the millennium witnessed a surge in power hitting, accompanied by controversies surrounding steroid use. Expansion introduced new teams, while contraction threatened the existence of others. The Montreal Expos' move to Washington symbolized both the potential and challenges faced by MLB in this dynamic era.

The Modern Game: Technology, Innovation, and the Future

In recent years, technology has woven itself into the fabric of baseball. Statcast, advanced analytics, and defensive shifts have altered the dynamics of the game. Yet, challenges such as extended game times have prompted the introduction of a pitch clock, underscoring the ongoing tension between tradition and progress.

Controversies and Accountability: The Astros Scandal and Beyond

The Astros sign-stealing scandal of 2017-2018 and subsequent revelations about the Red Sox underscored the challenges of maintaining fair play in the modern era. The fallout from these scandals raised questions about accountability and the league's commitment to preserving the integrity of the game.

A Shift in Landscapes: Franchise Moves and Realignment

Franchise moves, from the A's to Las Vegas in 2023, illustrate the ever-shifting landscapes of baseball. These moves echo a historical pattern of teams seeking new homes, reflecting the intricate dance between cities and franchises.

Uniforms: From Tradition to Innovation

The evolution of baseball uniforms mirrors the broader transformations within the sport. From the Knickerbockers' wool and straw hats to the modern era's technological partnerships, uniforms are not just clothing; they are symbols of baseball's journey through time.

Conclusion: A Tapestry Unfurls, Ever Evolving

As we conclude this odyssey through the history of Major League Baseball, we find ourselves standing at the crossroads of tradition and innovation, nostalgia and progress. Baseball's tapestry, woven with the threads of triumphs and challenges, tells a story that transcends the confines of a stadium.

In the echoes of historic moments, from Ruth's mighty swing to Robinson's defiant stand, we discern the heartbeat of a sport that mirrors the ebb and flow of American life. The journey through integration, expansion, scandals, and technological advancements reveals a game that adapts, learns, and perseveres.

As we look to the future, the echoes of the past resonate. Baseball, with its timeless allure, continues to captivate new generations. In the complex dance between tradition and change, baseball remains a living legacy—an enduring testament to the spirit of resilience and the boundless possibilities that unfold between the bases.

Thank You for Embarking on This Baseball Odyssey

As we close the final chapter of "The History of Major League Baseball," we extend our heartfelt gratitude for joining us on this captivating journey through the annals of America's pastime. Your dedication to exploring the highs and lows, triumphs and tribulations, has made this odyssey all the more meaningful.

Baseball, with its timeless allure, connects generations, weaving a tapestry of stories that transcend the boundaries of time and space. Whether you're a die-hard fan, a casual observer, or a newcomer to the world of baseball, we appreciate the time you've dedicated to delving into the rich history of the sport.

In the echoes of Babe Ruth's mighty swing, Jackie Robinson's courageous strides, and the crack of a well-hit ball resonates the collective heartbeat of a nation. Your journey through the evolution of uniforms, the expansion of franchises, and the seismic shifts in the game's dynamics reflects the broader narrative of American culture.

As the final inning of this literary ballgame approaches, we hope you've found moments of joy, reflection, and discovery within these pages. Baseball is more than a game; it's a mirror reflecting the soul of a nation, with all its complexities, challenges, and triumphs.

Our gratitude extends beyond the lines of this book to each reader who has embraced the spirit of the game. May the stories of baseball continue to inspire, entertain, and serve as a bridge connecting past, present, and future.

Thank you for sharing this baseball odyssey with us. May your love for the game endure, and may the crack of the bat and the roar of the crowd echo in your heart long after the final page.

If you enjoyed this book, please consider leaving a review by clicking here.

In the spirit of sportsmanship and camaraderie, James Bren.

Other Books by James Bren

The History of MMA

The History of the NFL

The History of the NHL and the Stanley Cup

The History of the UFC – Book 1

111 Weird, Fun, and Random *Facts About the UFC*

The History of the NHL

The History of Bellator

The History of the NBA

The History of the UFC – Book 2. *Coming soon!*

Printed in Great Britain
by Amazon

5c65aa5c-5f4b-4cdc-b893-31fe7f062b6bR01